PMP/PMBOK
100 Success Secrets

PMP/PMBOK 100 Success Secrets - Project
Management Professional; The Missing Exam
Study, Certification Preparation and Project
Management Body of Knowledge Guide Application
Guide

Gerard Blokdijk

PMP/PMBOK 100 Success Secrets

Copyright © 2008 by Gerard Blokdijk

PMP/PMBOK 100 Success Secrets
Gerard Blokdijk

There has never been a PMP/PMBOK manual like this.

100 Success Secrets is *not* about the ins and outs of PMP/PMBOK . Instead, it answers the top 100 questions that we are asked and those we come across in forums, our consultancy and education programs. It tells you exactly how to deal with those questions, with tips that have never before been offered in print.

This book is also *not* about PMP/PMBOK 's best practice and standards details. Instead it introduces everything you want to know to be successful with PMP/PMBOK .

Table of Contents

The Innovation of 2000 PMBOK

The 2000 PMBOK provides an upgraded manual for project managers. It is the new bible which project managers should know and have always handy in setting out their team tasks and upon leading a new project.

Just after the first few pages, the Introduction can still be found. This part provides readers with a brief overview of the book. It also sets the pace on what readers can most likely expect with the newly upgraded version.

The 2000 PMBOK also has the following segments within it:

1. Project Definition and Its Sub context

2. The PMBOK Lifecycle – This still contains the five main processes which governs project management.

3. Feasibility of Methods– The segment attempts to discuss how the project can actually cope up with different methods acquired. This gives readers a chance to compare and contrast between differing methods.

4. Current Technology and Art – As a new upgrade of the 2000 PMBOK, it already provides with technological innovations regarding project handling. Aside from manual resources, the book also talks about new programs available for making project schedules among others.

5. Standards and Ethical Procedures – Apart from emphasizing quality and efficiency, this book's segment also inculcates the value of observing project management ethics during task accom-

plishment. A set of standards is clearly handed out for readers to remember upon project handling. Ethics are also considered under this segment.

Under the close guidance of PMI, the 2000 PMBOK has been developed to suit the changing times of the fast-paced world of project management.

PMBOK Is Not Just An Acronym

What is a PMBOK? It is Project Management Body of Knowledge. Here's a guide to the PMBOK.

Apart from being a guide to the project management body of knowledge, the PMBOK is also being used by main organizations like the Fujitsu and the Boeing Aircraft. The book includes a process which just makes sure that the project has been defined properly, will be managed thoroughly, and accomplished with ease.

Since the contents it has are being widely accepted, all project managers must have it. The processes it has been proven to be effective in the field and ensures success.

The book is quite an easy read. It has a clear path which readers can take on from beginning until the end. So as you go along and read the book, you can easily identify the expectations and the important requirements you must have to arrive to a successful project. It also contains a useful method you can utilize to have a full grasp of a certain project. As a result, you end up identifying its expanse as wells as the schedule you need to build in ensuring that everything will be covered. You will also learn about project costs and how to seek the right resources.

In addition, it also tells you what level of understanding you must have with a certain project to prevent getting yourself into unnecessarily stressful situations. It also provides useful tips and know-hows. In many ways, PMBOK is really more than just a guide to the project management book of knowledge.

Should I Undergo A Certification Course PMP?

To pass the PMP accreditation exam, you need to have the proper training. This means pursuing the right certification course PMP training sessions. One way to take such training is to go online and participate in online training courses in Project Management.

Every online training provider will have their own specific pre-training requirements but most likely you will be asked to provide proof that you have gained Project Management experience for some time or are currently working in a job that requires Project Management skills. To be considered adequately trained by such Project Management training providers, you should be able to prove your technical knowledge and managerial capabilities have improved due to the training. Some people, due to the nature of their work, already have quite a lot of exposure to Project Management but just need some formal training for certification purposes (because no accreditation institution will be able to comprehensively measure your level of exposure any other way.)

You will find that investing in training under certification course PMP training sessions pays off pretty well in the end – because the compensation level for a Project Management Professional stands at the estimated median earning level of $70,000. One aspect of work as a Project Management Professional is that you have to stay up to date about any governmental regulations or laws that will designate the parameters of the project you will be working on. Though the hours are long in this work (with you being on call sometimes round the clock), the employment prospects seem pretty stable anyway which is good for job security.

The Benefits of PMP Certification Training

Project Management Professional (PMP) is one of the major certifications needed in boosting a professional's career in project management. This will help practitioners and students to have a powerful credential that can take them to a better career in project management. Before anyone can do that, project managers should take certification trainings to enhance their skills.

Management skills in handling team members are also tackled in PMP training. In project management, team building and goal setting are very important aspects of project management. The project manager must learn how to influence people especially the team members. Aside from that, handling conference and meetings are some of the major duties of project managers. They need to know the necessary methods to conduct a productive meeting.

Meeting Management skill is also discussed in PMP training to aid professionals in setting an effective goal in conferences. Also, communication skill in project management is needed to be an effective project manager. PMP certification training conducts this to help professionals keep a good relationship with other members of the team without compromising their leadership in managing the projects.

To get PMP certification trainings, professionals can avail of PMP classroom based trainings, Computer Based Training CBT, audio/ video CD's and boot camps. These options in PMP certification trainings will certainly aid project managers who have busy schedules and endless deadlines to finish. These options will provide convenience to practitioners anywhere they are. PMP certification training can assist the students in getting the right planning tools for the project.

Download PMBOK: The Evident Increase in the Usage

The evident increase in the usage of Internet for information gathering presented more and more ways in which users of this information can access them.

The difficulty of the PMP Certification Examination is no secret to anyone. And all the past-takers lament of this fact. This is probably why more and more people engaged in taking the Examination are going to great lengths as to get all the information they need to ensure their passing, which further exemplifies the goal of having a pass and not a failure.

This is so apparent with the increasing numbers of Internet Sites offering downloadable PMBOK to the applicants. And the number of these Websites is not decreasing, but rather they are steadily increasing.

There are Websites that offers these PMBOK for a specified fee that comes in as a cost-worthy expense to try. Some Websites require the users to first register into their accounts before being able to download the documents, while there are also those that offer these for free to their members to enjoy and download.

There are also those that give them for free, but already there are many former users that argue that the information inside them is quite worthless or at least irrelevant to the PMP Certification Examination.

What is apparent is that caution must be extended by the people doing the downloading into ensuring that the document to be downloaded are critically sufficient for their needs. For one,

Websites should criticize thoroughly for their credibility in information giving before a downloading is started.

In the goal to pass one of the hardest Certification Examinations ever made by PMI, time is crucial to both reviewing and answering and should not be wasted by irrelevant or useless information.

Finding a Free Download of PMBOK Risk Management Process

Individuals can now get a free download of PMBOK Risk Management process just by doing a simple search on the internet. A free download on PMBOK risk management process can help a candidate in his studies for the PMP exam certification. The PMBOK guide, published by PMI, identifies the essential principles, processes and knowledge of project management which are generally accepted by the different industries and disciplines worldwide. The PMBOK third edition is the latest revision of the PMBOK and supersedes PMBOK 2000. The PMBOK divides project management into nine knowledge areas and one of them is Project Risk Management.

Project Risk Management aims to reduce or eliminate risks inherent in any project undertaking so that it can be properly handled, controlled, managed, mitigated, and/or avoided. A free download of PMBOK Risk Management process is an essential tool for candidates of PMP exam certifications who are on a budget and cannot afford the expensive books, CDs and online courses offered by other companies.

A free download of PMBOK Risk Management process contains almost as much review material as the actual exam preparation materials that are sold online or in bookstores. There may be some limitations on free downloads like topics that do not really provide a good explanation of a subject or topics that do not provide a review for the courses discussed. These can easily be remedied by looking for more free downloads on PMBOK Risk Management process. The more review materials an individual has, the more comprehensive his studies will be on the Risk Management process.

What to Look for in A Free PMP Sample Test

Sample tests are in proliferation nowadays. No matter what type of certification or licensure you need to take, you can always assure your success through the use of sample tests. Various kinds are available online.

If you want a detailed fix of what's it like to undergo the actual one, sample tests are available online as you make a purchase. But if you want to just pair it up with the current study materials, there are also various free downloads currently available online.

Even free PMP sample tests are now in proliferation. A free PMP sample test would surely catch your attention as you surf online to get more information about the PMP. Moreover, a free PMP sample test would most likely appear on your screen when you scout online for study materials. But from all these free choices, which one should you take?

A good free PMP sample test must contain questions about initiating projects. This is corollary to project management. The PMP would require assessing knowledge when it comes to project recognition and the confidence a project manager has when it comes to leading a course of action.

A good free PMP sample test also has questions pertaining to proper project planning.

This is the lifeblood of any project since this is the structure in which everything and everyone would refer to through the course of the project. Proper project planning must be exemplified by good project managers.

So if you are scouting for the best free PMP sample test, make sure that these essentials are met. Even if it offered for free, you should still be worthy of downloading and spending some time referring to it.

Choose The Best Free PMP Test

Preparing for the PMP exam day is already a breeze nowadays. There are various ways you could adapt before you can actually go into the exam room and bag that PMP certificate.

Among all of the methods available nowadays, what seems to be the best form yet are the trial tests. These materials aim to simulate the exam itself and promise to provide reviewers with the similar feel they can get upon answering the actual PMP certification exam.

They are usually available in stores and various book shops. However, changing times also made things a lot easier for all of us. There are plenty of websites online which offer programs and downloads for a fee. These programs are also trial tests and simulated exams which can help you on your way to the exam day.

What's more is that there are already free PMP test available online. These free PMP test are easily downloadable and easy to follow. Although they are indeed wonderful, especially since they help you save up on the costs, there are a few things you need to remember in choosing the best free PMP test.

Consider the program itself. Look at the specifics it promises to achieve. Analyze if it really covers the right project management guidelines and if it is also in multiple choice format.

Take a look at the credentials of the distributor. Is it something you have always been familiar with or a techie newbie? Also, do they boast of PMP approval?

Check the system requirements as well. Don't fall for a free PMP test that promises good things but for a sizeable hard disk space. You never know what those extra space would actually be for.

Finding a Study Guide on PMP Project Management Professional

Having a Project Management Professional (PMP) certificate is a good credential for anyone who wants to further their careers in project management. Passing the Project Management Professional exam given by the Project Management Institute qualifies an individual to be a PMP. The exam is based on the PMP Book of Knowledge (PMPBOK) also which is PMI's ANSI standard. Passing the PMP certification exam can be a very challenging task for any individual and getting a study guide on PMP will certainly help them in passing the PMP certification exam.

There are several study guides on PMP project management professional. Some individuals still prefer the book-style of reviewing for the exam instead of going online to study or downloading a computer based training material. This is because a paperback edition of a PMP project management professional study guide can easily be accessed by anyone, anytime, anywhere without having to plug the computer and going online. They can also forego of bringing along expensive, bulky, and sometimes heavy notebook computers just to study their lessons.

Getting a PMP project management professional study guide is essential in a candidate's review for PMI's PMP certification exam. These books are an easier option for many people because it uses real-world scenarios rather than the traditional study guide offered by the PMBOK. With real-world situations, candidates are more likely to understand the principles and processes of project management. Most paperback books offer assessment exams with review questions to test a candidate's readiness for the actual exam. A good book will also have a comprehensive practice exam that mimic the actual PMP and CAPM certification exam.

Tips to Use for Passing the PMP Accreditation Exam

The PMP exam is quite a long exam to take – this is why you are given four hours within which to answer the 200 computer-based questions supplied to each examinee.

To pass, you have to be able to answer at least 137 of these 200 questions correctly (which is equivalent to a percentile score of 68.5%.) Of course, any potential employer would want to see you get a much higher score than that to hire you – and the job market can be merciless due to the numbers of people you may be competing against for the same position. So always aim to get the best possible score you can get.

One thing that should help you is that the actual PMP exam may have questions that contain superfluous information. This superfluous information actually will not help you get the right answer to that particular question (and perhaps were inserted just to test how analytical you are.)

Another thing to look out for would be a question that seems to have more than one correct answer offered to you. In reality, there is only one totally correct answer per question on the real exam. The trick is to weed out any seemingly correct answers from the true one.

Try to use the perspective of an actual PMP (Project Management Professional) when trying to answer the real exam questions. Some examinees make the mistake of trying to answer with information from a layman point of view (which is wrong.) The exam questions are testing your ability to think like a PMP.

Lastly, scrutinize answers which use words that generalize (such as must, never, always, and completely) because these may be trick answers that can be misleading.

Comparing PMBOK 2000 with PMBOK Third Edition

The Project Management Professional (PMP) is a certified individual by the Project Management Institute (PMI). PMI was established to standardize the project management best practices so that it can be applied into any discipline--from the IT industry to the construction industry. In 1987, PMI published a white paper which was known as the Project Management Book of Knowledge or PMBOK. Since then, the PMBOK has gone through three stages of revisions. The latest one, the PMBOK third edition supersedes the PMBOK 2000 which was published as the second edition of the very popular PMBOK guide.

PMI and ANSI set a clear definition and description of the best practices in the PMBOK 2000 guide. The guide includes knowledge and practices that are applicable to most projects from any industry and ensures that the projects are implemented within the time limit and within the specified budget. PMBOK 2000 has been replaced by the PMBOK third edition thanks to the various recommendations and improvements given to PMI. In PMBOK 2000, the following were revised and/or improved.

Most noticeable in the changes would be the physical ones. Compared to PMBOK 2000, the PMBOK third edition has a new cover page, is 174 pages thicker, has better and improved illustrations and graphics and the application, implementation and revelation of best practices is in boldface for easy reference. Another big change from the PMBOK 2000 is that PMI has also introduced new sections on project management and has clarified several concepts and introduced new techniques in the PMBOK third edition.

Introduction to PMBOK 2004

The Project Management Book of Knowledge or PMBOK 2004 contains the essential principles, processes and knowledge for the successful implementation and management of any project. The PMBOK 2004 also includes several proven best practices that are widely used by different industries and disciplines. With valuable contributions from certified members, the PMI reintroduced the PMBOK 2000 second edition. PMBOK 2004 was released and supersedes the PMBOK 2000 second edition guide to project management.

The PMBOK 2004 guide aims to identify the generally recognized good practices of project and program management applicable to all fields of study and industry from the IT to construction. Exhaustive studies and explanations are excluded and only the knowledge and practices that are applicable to most projects most of the time are included in the discussion. These principles, practices and processes have been proven to be accepted and recognized by the different industries and will increase the chances of a successful implementation of a project. The PMBOK 2004 identifies the project management team as the one responsible for the implementation of a project and identifying what is appropriate for it.

The PMBOK 2004 guide provides a foundation for basic reference and is recommended reading for individuals wishing to take the Certified Associate in Project Management (CAPM), the Project Management Professional (PMP), and the Program Management Professional (PgMP) exam certification, the Project Management education and training, and other accreditation programs in project management. The PMBOK 2004 guide is also recommended reading for Senior Executives and Managers, Project/Program Managers, Stakeholders, Consultants, Educators, Trainers, Project Team Members, and any other individual involved in project management.

The PMBOK Lifecycle--The Core of PMP

The PMBOK is a must-have for every project manager. It contains all knowledge which server as precursors to proper management of various projects.

The PMBOK lifecycle is actually made up of five important steps towards effective project management.

First step – Initiating involves the project manager himself and him solely. In this step, he begins to authorize the start of a project and proceeds on to commit himself and his team into accomplishing it. Initiating is what fires off the entire project management process.

Second step – Planning serves as the framework of the entire project. This defines the scope and the objectives to which the project should operate. This is also where a strict schedule is organized and deadlines would have to be included to assure that everything is done in a timely manner. This is usually done amongst the project manager and the entire team so that proper brainstorming can take place.

Third step – Executing is doing the project. This is where the first two steps come to life. However, quality assurance is key so that even though tight deadlines must be met, the team need not compromise the results of their hard work.

Fourth step – Monitoring and Controlling In here, stakeholders as well as sponsors also had to be included in these because other issues such as budget allocations and additional measures may come up from time to time, depending on the project owners.

The project manager and the team also has to consult these people prior to going about the whole process.

Fifth step – Closing This is not just ending the project but moreover, closing it by finalizing everything properly. This ensures that everything has been done according to plan without leaving anything unsettled.

How to Buy PMI PMP eBay-auctioned Materials

If you are aiming to buy PMI PMP accreditation preparation materials, then one place you can buy these would be at eBay. One advantage with doing this is that you are able to buy PMI PMP eBay-auctioned materials at a lower price (and sometimes with the shipping fee at a discounted rate or completely waived.)

Some titles you could opt to purchase from eBay under the PMI PMP category are: 15500 PMP PMI PMBOK PROJECT MANAGEMENT QUESTION , 15500 PMP PMI PMBOK QUESTIONS v RITA MULCAHY, PMP Project Management Exam PMBok Third Edition - PMI, PMP Project Management 11 Exam Prep Tests PMI, PMP GOLD PACKAGE 11000 PMI Explanation Study AID Exam, and PMP & CAPM Exam 35 Contact Hour Audio Seminar PMBOK PMI.

Under this same category (but from the eBay stores), you may purchase this title: PMP PMI-001 Exam QA latest practice questions & answers.

One disadvantage with using eBay though is that the products are put on the auction block only for a limited period of time. If you happen to buy them early, prices are usually at their highest (by eBay standards, that is.) Prices are in US dollars but if you want to check how that is computed or translated into your own home currency, you can use the Universal Currency Converter.

It is also advantageous to use eBay if you have something to sell that falls under the PMI PMP materials category.

Your 3 Point Guide to PMP Application

The PMP application can be a bit of a task, but it would all be worth it once you get your certificate.

Here are the important details which you must know and accomplish throughout the whole PMP application process.

1. Prepare a detailed resume. Since this is for PMP certification and not for employment, highlight only those which are related to project management. The authorities will look at these two important factors within your resume: educational attainment and work experience. Provide them with a detailed presentation of what your course was back in college and be sure to include all the majors you had pertaining to project management. This detail is greatly looked upon. As you go on to discuss your work experience within the paper, make sure that you also include the time frames wherein you have served as project manager. The time frame is deemed highly important.

2. As you pass the resume assessment, you should next review a code of professional conduct. This agreement assures you of ethical responsibilities as you go along the process. Upon signing this, you proceed to the next process.

3. This is already the PMP exam itself. This is a multiple-choice type of test which would assess how much you know about project management. This covers all the basics as well as the in-depth information only project managers are expected to know of. After passing this exam, that's the only time you will be eligible to receive the PMP certificate. This is of course the last part and the deciding factor for the entire PMP application process.

PMP Certificate: Out of the Ordinary

Some people may think that certificates really are not a big thing. They may go on thinking that a certificate is just a piece of paper and another addition to your credential but hardly goes noticed. But if you are aspiring for top level positions in big shot companies, you would find these line of thinking entirely false.

A PMP certificate is more than just a certificate.

The PMP certification was actually launched by the Project Management Institute. Nobody can just be authorized to take on the certification exam and even if you have been accepted to take it, that still does not guarantee that you would get your certification. It really takes a rather grueling process to get it but once you do, you'd realize how much it's all worth it.

Before you get approved, you would have to present your project management credentials first to the proper authorities. They will look at your educational attainment and how much of it has been focused on project management majors.

Then they would of course also see how actually experienced you are in the field of project management. Usually, they require eight years of first hand experience wherein you have served as a project manager yourself for a minimum of sixty months. Moreover, this means that you did not report to any other supervisor but led your own team into accomplishing different projects.

Once you get approved, the PMP certificate is still not easily within reach. You need to undergo the exam which would assess just how much you really know about project management. It involves the basics as well as the in-depth knowledge project managers should be aware of. The exam is what bags the PMP certifi-cate in the end.

Which PMP Certification Course Should I Take?

In an ideal world, we would have all the leisure time at our disposal to be able to study any topic we choose for as long as we wish. Unfortunately, this is not an ideal world so most of us have responsibilities that will limit the time we have for pursuing studies aside from work. But we know that we need to study in order to advance in our current profession – and that holds true as well for the Project Management Professional occupation.

Equally ideally, we would have the resources (like money for car fuel, or for transportation via mass transit) to be able to attend classroom sessions for the PMP Certification Course we need. But this may not always be feasible (like if we have to work from 8 to 5 in our present job to support ourselves and our families) so for those who cannot go to the classroom location, the classroom can come to you via online distance learning options instead.

Though the classroom sessions could provide more in-depth knowledge and skills to us, the online options are good too because they can zero in on the particular topics we are most interested in or need the most. So the advantage with a classroom session is you get more comprehensive training that leaves you a well-rounded Project Management Professional. The advantage with online sessions is that they weed out the surplus knowledge and help you focus on whatever knowledge and skills are most necessary to us. So it would be difficult to say which one is best, because that would be implying a one-size-fits-all approach is best. And in Project Management, that is never true.

The Advantage and Disadvantage of Using Blogs as Your PMP Dumps

Let us say you are someone aspiring to become a PMP (or Project Management Professional), and you are looking for some PMP dumps (or brain dumps as they are also known) to help you prepare for the PMP accreditation process and exam. Would any blogs be useful as your PMP dumps?

It would depend on the proficiency level of the person who created these blogs in the first place. The biggest disadvantage with a PMP dump or PMP brain dump is that you are limited by the intelligence level and skill sets of the person who wrote the material. This means that if the creator had a so-so mark on the PMP exam and is a mediocre Project Management Professional, it would probably be a bad idea to use his experience as your benchmark for training for your own accreditation exam. But if you choose someone who is a very good Project Management Professional (as proven by his work records and his PMP exam score, then it might be a good idea to use the blogs of that person to help you along too.

But, with the content of blogs (and this applies to all content of all blogs), you have to take the information supplied with a grain of salt: is this person telling the truth? You only have the word of the writer as your basis, so (unless you personally know this writer) you have to sieve through the advice of the person on his blog to find out what rings true and what sounds illogical and downright untrue.

This is also why some experts denounce the use of brain dumps altogether and advocate use of legitimate (albeit more expensive) PMP preparation material instead.

PMP Exam Cram: The CD with Meaningful Knowledge

The conception of Computers have brought into good use the knowledge and talents of all people.

They have now published books on so many things that information is now easy to come by. And the advent of the Computers has improved a lot the way in which information is passed from one person to another.

The Internet even improved it even more and to say the least, information gathering has gone from speech to Internet downloads, but there is another form of information gathering that entails too the use of computers.

It is through the use of CD's. Being one of the toughest Certification Examinations, the PMP has seen its share of information gathering and sharing methods deemed to make the Examination easier for the applicants. One of these is the PMP Exam Cram 2, which is offered on a CD. It is even available in the Internet for easy purchasing by the end-user.

It offers relevant and meaningful information in real-world scenarios and is presented in a manner that is friendly in style.

It is in fact a good extension and complement of Project Management Book of Knowledge or PMBOK. The CD is expected to help the applicants into remembering important concepts and ides.

Also, it provides meaningful knowledge on what topics the Examination is more likely to cover. Aside from these, it is also complete with a lot of tips on practice examinations. The Cram

Sheet for last minute review has made this CD program famous, which is a good way of training the users in terms of managing the question and answer under limited time.

PMP examfree: A Good Alternative for PMP Review

To have a Project Management Professional (PMP) certification, an individual must have the basic knowledge of the principles, code of conduct, techniques, methods and standards of project management. To be highly competitive in today's business industry, project managers must gain the skills in controlling resources and knowing the different standards in project management.

PMP practice examfree online can help individuals in equipping them with the proper concepts and standards that is acceptable in businesses. PMP practice examfree will help test the knowledge of professionals in handling proper decision making, managing team members and creating resource control. There are several alternatives in gaining a good training in project management. Audio/ video trainings, study guides and free practice exams will prepare professionals in passing the PMP certification test.

Companies these days search for candidates that can meet their particular education requirements. Aside from the fact that job experience plays a great part in proving one's capability, credentials are also equally important to secure the job position in project management. To do that, professionnals should take time in getting themselves PMP practice examfree to train them in real certification test environment. This also provides multiple choice and fill in the blank type of examination.

This exam is a great tool to practice PMP exam anytime; and it's for free! Professionals just need to look for new editions and versions of PMP examfree to them with an accurate and updated skill in project management. PMP examfree online is definitely a great way to start preparing for the certification test.

PMP FASTrack – Your Certification Buddy

Before you go into the PMP exam, certainly you'd need to review and prep yourself up for the looming day. There are various now available to help you with this such as flash cards, study guides, and even training courses. All of these methods are really helpful, but there's one thing that quite stands out from the pack.

And these are trial exams.

Trial exams have always been heavily utilized by any kind of licensure or certification exam, not just for PMP alone. Usually, all the other methods mentioned above work side by side trial exams to help get you on your way into being succeful with the actual exam.

This is where PMP FASTrack comes in.

PMP FASTrack is more than just the usual trial exam. This program actually simulates the PMP certification exam itself. The software was developed by Rita Mulcahy for PMP purposes.

The exam is psychometrically accurate, which is why it is generally trusted and proven. The PMP FASTrack covers almost every detail of the actual exam, except of course the actual questions itself. What it does is to simulate the topics which the actual exam covers so that once you get into the real exam, you would definitely become more familiar with what type of questions would you most likely expect as you go along.

By using the PMP FASTrack, you will be able to grasp important concepts and key words as easily as you would through the use of flash cards. You will have an idea about knowing only what's

important with your study guides instead of forcing to learn everything before the exam day.

What is a PMP Fastrack 5 Simulation Product?

An accredited PMP (Project Management Professional) named Rita Mulcahy created a PMP Fastrack 5 simulation product called the PM FASTrack PMP Exam Simulation Software (Version 5) with the assistance of a psychometrician. This means the product (which is composed of 1400 questions) is remarkably similar to the genuine PMP accreditation exam itself. You may take the questions based on whether they fall under the PMP simulation, Super PMP simulation, certain keywords and/or concepts, process group, or knowledge area categories of Project Management.

The question bank of the PM FASTrack PMP Exam Simulation Software (Version 5) can be automatically upgraded if your personal computer has Internet access. Exam reporting then archiving can also be upgraded through this product. The product can also provide questions that are worded in a manner which may be quite similar to the questions in the real exam. And since the point of taking simulation exams is to anticipate the real exam questions, this makes it advantageous for you.

You can also use the RMCs PMP Exam Prep Textbook to bone up on any exam questions in this product which may have confused you or that you found too difficult.

The PM FASTrack PMP Exam Simulation Software (Version 5) can be used on personal computers that are fitted with a CD Rom drive (if you will be using the CD version); Administrator usage privileges; a processor of 600 MHz Intel Pentium III standard (or an equivalent product); 32- bit Windows XP or Windows 2000; at least 128 megabytes of RAM (though it is advisable to use 250 megabytes for best results); available disk space maxing out at 100 megabytes; and Internet access so you can get upgrades for your product registration and question databank.

The PMP Exam Preparation Kit—Still Making PMP News

PMP news all over the world is now talking about a breakthrough in PMP preparation, through the advent of exam preparation kits offered by PMP.

Since its inception last 2006, the exam preparation kit was the predecessor of all sample tests which are now proliferating the market. Ever since the PMP news, the exam kit has taken the PMP certification world by storm.

The kit offers reviewers a chance to be briefed through the use of a thousand different questions all spread out to cover the necessary processes of project management. It also includes five different mock exams as well as the breeze of revision through 180 quick notes. The kit also offers useful tips and tricks which can help the taker on the day of PMP certification exam.

It was on every PMP news because primarily, it was approved by the PMI. It is also a highly interactive software which users can easily manipulate and navigate through. A virtual mentor can also assist users while they try to go about the use of the software. Quick FAQ's are also easy to access within the program.

In partnership with Whizlabs, the PMP exam preparation kit has been launched. Whizlabs has always been known to efficiently accomplish the task of producing certification preparation materials for reviewers. They specialize in the field of software development. Since the PMP only wants the best for their reviewers, partnering with Whizlabs is definitely the best choice.

And ever since its creation, the exam preparation kit still continues to make PMP news and become regarded as the forefather of all PMP sample tests which then followed suit.

PMP PMI: The Project Management Institute

Many have asked on the nature of the Project Management Institute, which is more commonly known and referred to as PMI.

It is sad to note that only the people in the world of Project Management are able to understand its importance in the quest to ensure the maintenance of the quality and credibility of the Project Managers.

It is a very crucial organization, which is considered and accepted as a globally recognized Certification in the world of Project Management.

In fact, its Certification Examinations are being used and outlined as benchmarks by the all Project Managers. They have also been known as to having implemented and offered one of the toughest Certification Examinations. In its entirety, the PMI offers three levels of Certification Examination for Project Managers. These Examinations differ in terms of the levels of the questions, toughness and ranking.

The first is given to members of Project Management teams, while the seconds are for the Project Manager themselves. The third is considered as the hardest and is named as Program Management Professional and is offered to Project Managers, who seek the last, highest and the hardest form of Certification in Project Management.

They are most often to be found in the top echelons of the Business itself and while it is certainly the hardest and highest form, the second level of Certification, which is the Project Management Professional or PMP, is currently the most sought after Certification. And is originally and critically based on the standards set under the PMP Examination Specification, which is in turn made by the PMI in 2005.

The Advantages of PMP Practice Tests

The Project Management Professional (PMP) is one of the best certifications that benefits project managers and professionals. This certification proved to be a great advantage in having a good credential and resume. To earn the PMP title, one must take PMP trainings, study guides and practice tests. This will assist professionals in getting the right preparation.

A PMP practice test is a very important aspect of PMP review. It will help them in obtaining the skills and knowledge in the different standards, concepts and techniques in project management. Practice test provides students various options and additional test exercises that will surely enhance the knowledge of professionals. The PMP certification test requires rigid training and study in order to pass. This also gives professionals a comprehensive coverage of the PMP exam objectives. A PMP practice test bases its questions on the Project Management Body of Knowledge or PMBOK published by PMI to have accurate questionnaire.

On this test, there are free work books that are given to students to aid them with the knowledge in answering the diagram and chart questions. Hands on exercises are essential to give examinees a view on what real practical projects would look like. These exercises will help solve real problems that professionals encounter in managing projects.

PMP practice exams are essential review materials for workers and professionals who want to take the PMP certification exam and further their careers in project management. PMP practice exams can help in the self-evaluation of individuals in the assessment of their readiness for the actual exams.

PMP Makes a Real Project Manager

PMP is not just all about certification. PMP is made under the premise of acknowledging what makes a real project manager worthy of the title. Beyond skills, beyond professionalism, PMP aims to build a project manager reputation based on the following factors:

1. A project manager inspires his people and shares with the group's vision. He does not just lead to execute plans, but leads under the plan's vision. His goal is the same as that of his members, which is why he is looked up to by the team and is treated as an inspiration.

2. A project manager knows how to communicate with all of the members of his team regardless of level. He can clearly communicate his plans and ideas with his team and makes sure that everybody else understands it.

3. Actions speak louder than words. Therefore, a project manager must enforce integrity in everything he does. He should also serve as the ethical model of his co-workers.

4. Enthusiasm should also be displayed by the project manager. Humor and optimism does a lot to motivate employees especially during the most difficult times. Leaders who are filled with enthusiasm always bring a can-do attitude within the workplace.

5. A project manager must know how to properly delegate tasks not just for the purpose of having everybody else work. The tasks must be delegated in such a way that everyone does a work under his specialization. Tasking should fit an employee's job description so that efficiency would always be above standards.

These are the other factors shaped by PMP. Project managers would not just benefit from PMP by certification alone. It also brings in a lot of important know-how and realization as to how they should act as "real" project managers.

What are the Responsibilities of a PMP Project Manager?

Like the term and acronym indicate, a PMP Project Manager is basically someone who knows how to manage projects and has earned the accreditation of being a Project Management Professional to show that capability.

One of the responsibilities of a PMP Project Manager is to hold project management training for the rest of the team at his work. For instance, if he is a Project Manager for a construction site, then that means most likely the other members of the construction project have no idea what Project Management is all about and how it will affect implementation of the construction project objectives and the expected outcome.

When you have attained the accreditation of being a Project Management Professional (PMP), the most obvious expectation is that you can manage projects for your employer or organization much better than anyone else. And the definition of better, as applied this way, means minimizing or even eliminating as much possibilities of failure as possible by using the best possible Project Management techniques and tools at your disposal.

Another responsibility of a PMP Project Manager is that you need to be able to identify the past, present, and potential risks that your current project faced, is facing, and will be facing in the near and distant future. Once you have seen the risks, you can then make an educated discussion as to whether to hire a risk management professional on whom you can unload the risk management aspect, or simply face and manage these project risks yourself with help from your team.

Finding a PMP Question

Finding a PMP question on its nine knowledge areas is relatively easy because there are many websites and online schools offering PMP certification preparation lessons and kits. These online schools help individuals prepare themselves for the PMP certification exam. The Project Management Professional PMP certification exam is an exam given by the Project Management Institute and qualifies an individual as capable of successfully managing and implementing a project. The PMP certification exam is a difficult exam and is widely recognized all over the world.

A quick search on the net on a PMP question sample will give millions of results. There are many legal websites that provide a sample PMP question for a candidate to answer. This marketing strategy is intended to entice an individual to buy or enroll in their PMP classes. A PMP question listed in the website enables an individual to see the benefits of taking online courses on project management. It is a well known fact that online courses are now a trend for busy professionals and businessmen wanting to further their skills and knowledge on project management.

There are also illegal websites that contain braindumps on various certifications which, unfortunately, also includes a PMP question or set of questions. These braindumps are an illegal source of information because they contain actual PMP exam questions which have somehow been stolen and published. A braindump devaluates the essence of getting a certification because many unqualified individuals are getting their certifications because of this practice. Reviewing and studying a PMP question via a braindump will only make the exam certifications even harder to pass.

Why Should I Use PMP Sample Questions?

Since the PMP certification (or Project Management Professional certification) should be based on certain Project Management objectives, namely, Initiating, Planning, Executing, Controlling, Closing, and Professional Responsibility, any PMP exam preparation guide you get should offer PMP sample questions that will meet these objectives separately or in conjunction.

Any PMP sample questions you try to answer – in the final analysis – ought to help you try to prepare adequately for the PMP accreditation exam. So choose a PMP exam preparation specialist who will explain to you in detail what you need to understand when you seem to make mistakes. The detailed explanations will help in clarifying difficult concepts for you so that you will no longer make the same mistakes over and over again. So, the value of PMP sample questions lies in the explanations supplied to you after you encounter such PMP sample questions.

Sometimes, it is a good idea to network with those who have already undergone the PMP accreditation exam before you so that they can give you their own interpretation of the answers to PMP sample questions. There are currently forums on the Internet which you can join so you can chat for free with experienced PMPs who can help you.

When you are scouting around for exam preparation specialists who may offer you PMP sample questions, be careful about buying any PMP sample questions or guides. Not all creators of such sample questions and guides have permission to publish their work or they may have literally lifted the questions from real PMP exams which then counts as copyright infringement.

PMP Study Guides: A Great Help in PMP Review

A career in project management is a demanding job. It requires several skills in managing people, resources, cases and projects. Especially in the field of construction and software development, accurate planning is necessary to have a positive outcome in project management. That is why Project Management Professional or PMP certification is needed to provide practitioners and students a chance to study and improve their skills in management. This certification has helped in providing prestigious credentials and skills for professionals in different business fields.

In order to have a better future in project management, practitioners should seriously consider getting trainings that will equip them in their career. To make that possible, students can use PMP study guides to provide them with proper training in standards and concepts of project management. This includes a full coverage of the test objectives and additional workbook to help master the skills in answering diagrams and charts. Study guides also provide hands on experience and exercises to strengthen the important skills that will also be used in actual job environment. Apart from that, there are also stimulating review questions on every section to prepare for the real test.

PMP study guides are not limited to provide test questions and reading materials. There are also electronic flashcards, audio and video instruction CDs that can help professionals in getting the needed training for project management. Now professionals can choose whatever type of medium will best fit their lifestyle. PMP study guides will absolutely help in obtaining their certification in project management.

An Overview on Project Management Institute's PMBOK guide

The Project Management Institute is the initiator of the leading organization in project management and the author of Project Management Body of Knowledge or PMBOK. This association is known in 160 countries and has over 240,000 members. PMI has helped in supporting the business industry by providing professional standards in project management. Project Management Institute is also active in performing research, participating in advocacies to the profession and giving businesses an access to resources and information.

This organization started in 1969. The founders of this association realized the importance of distributing process information, networking and solving common problems in project management. The Project Management Institute created PMBOK to help project managers, practitioners and professionals in various business fields. This guide is a great tool to identify the different knowledge areas and essential processes of project management. Aside from that, it also discusses the best practices and procedures to successfully execute projects in various disciples.

Project Management Institute established the PMBOK guide that became a recognized standard all over the world. This document gives a fundamental concept on managing projects in engineering, automotive, software, IT, construction and other industries. The PMBOK guide has helped several businesses in providing them the basic knowledge on how to initiate, execute, plan, monitor, control and close a particular project. To be able to get a certification in project management, professionals must be able to review and study the PMBOK to equip them with the necessary skills and knowledge in PMP. This will definitely give them the fundamental concept project management.

What is the Global Value of Project Management PMP Accreditation?

Training for Project Management PMP status has become more advantageous because the ISO (International Organization for Standardization) organization has granted ISO/IEC 17024 status to the PMP certification system run by the Project Management Institute. The ISO/IEC 17024 accreditation for the PMP accreditation system by the Geneva, Switzerland-based ISO accreditation body is fairly unique among accreditation systems. ISO helped make the Project Management Institute system more acceptable to employers all over the world by raising the credibility of PMP accreditation.

In turn, the other Project Management accreditation systems of the Project Management Institute also benefit because the Project Management Institute relies on the same development system, maintenance system, and quality management system for each and every Project Management credential. So whether you are starting out in Project Management by aiming for CAPM (or Certified Associate in Project Management) status; PgMP (or Program Management Professional) status; OPM3 (Organizational Project Management Maturity Model); or simply PMP status, you know that the ISO accreditation will hold for all these anyway.

The Project Management Institute has been operating for over 38 years in the field of Project Management certification – so aside from the current ISO certification, it has all those years of experience in training people in Project Management concepts and skills. Even as a nonprofit, the Project Management Institute is considered the world leader in expertise in Project Management at the moment. So if you pursue PMP status, it shows that you are committed to professionalism in Project Management and its real world practices.

The PMP Exam: How to pass on your first try?

For all those wanting to pass the PMP, the applicants would direly need to enroll and study a lot of readings and papers about the Certification Examination.

They all know the hardship in answering the questions posted in it. In fact, this Examination is one of the most difficult ever concocted by PMI.

In real terms, passing the Examination is a crucial matter, especially for those who have taken it again and again. But for those who have to take it as first-timers, there is a rather more effective way of studying that promises to be worthwhile. Already there is a book entitled, The PMP Exam: How to Pass On Your First Try, and it is quite a well-read book for all those aspiring to pass the PMP Certification Examination.

The book is earmarked as a self-study guide specially-made for PMP Examinations with information about processes numbering 44 in all, and 592 inputs, outputs and the tools in Project Management.

The book also contains in its pages, PMP insider information kept secret and detailed explanations of all PMP subjects. As for the questions that befuddled all applicants, the book offers tips on how to spot and avoid these test tricks. They, the applicants, are also given examples of hundreds of highly realistic sample questions that might appear in the Certification Examination. These are expected to strengthen their understanding of PMP concepts, which could ultimately add up to the reasons on how they were able to pass the Examination in just one sitting.

What is PMP: The Requirements

The PMP is also known as the Project Management Professional, which was conceptualized as a Certification by the Project Management Institute, which tries to uplift and increase the efficiency and talents of the Project Managers worldwide through its Certification Examination.

It is a very critical Certification that is given only to those who have passed the PMP Certification Examination. Before the Examination, the applicants must first have the necessary requirements in order for them to be able to avail of the Examination.

The requirements are many and they begin by requiring a high school diploma on the part of the applicant. A Project Management Professional must also have an accomplished and specific educational attainment and years of experience.

There is also a code of professional conduct that all must adhere to. In terms of the Certification Examination, the applicant must be able to pass it. The Examination is intended as an objectively created way that allows the PMI to assess and measure the knowledge of Project Manager In case of a failure of the PMP holders to retain these requirements, they would stand to lose the Certification they've been awarded.

Also the applicants must have performed the jobs of a Project Manager over time of 60 months within 8 years. The applicant must have finished a whole 35 hours of education that is directly connected with the teachings in Project Management, but in cases where there are applicants, who already possess a bachelor's degree, they only require about 4,500 (hrs) and an accumulated 36 months of experience.

Getting Advanced Project Management Training and PMP Products Exam Preparation Online

Every organization engages in a project. That is why they need individuals who are adept at project management so that they may be able to complete their task on time and within budget. The Project Management Professional (PMP) is a crucial part of a project manager's career. This will gauge an individual's ability in handling projects. This will also determine the individual's determination to advance the skills and knowledge in project management.

There are products that can give advanced project management training and PMP exam that helps develop management and organizational skills of project managers. These days, where companies strive to be on top, it is important to invest on trainings that will help project managers in advancing their skills and provide them with the latest strategies in project management.

There are three levels of certification for project management that start off with the CAPM or the Certified Associate in Project Management. This is the basic level of project management and is intended for project team members.

The PMP is the second level and is intended for project managers. The PMP is also considered as the standard of all project management certifications. Advanced project management training PMP products for exam preparation can be obtained from various sources.

There are now several schools that offer advanced project management training and PMP products for exam preparation. These schools usually have online training courses for project management that give the individual the advantage of getting the training for PMP exam without ever leaving the workplace or disrupting the work schedule.

Should I Use a Brain Dump PMP Guide?

A Brain Dump PMP guide is basically any document that will help you prepare for the Project Management Professional (or PMP) certification exam. The PMP accreditation is administered by the Project Management Institute to help professionals gain project management expertise recognition. Actually, even simple handwritten notes by someone who has taken the PMP exam before qualify as a brain dump. In its most literal sense, a brain dump is the act of your writing down anything you know about a particular topic.

To be considered for the PMP exam, you need to prove you have had minimum experience of at least 4500 hours in Project Management, plus have trained in this field in classroom sessions for at least 35 hours.

If you use the handwritten notes of some one you know - who gave these to you for free – then it would be legal to use those notes. However, once you start buying brain dumps, then you have to be careful because some creators of brain dumps actually trespass on the intellectual property rights of the original accreditation exams. Some people may even go to the extent of copying the content of original accreditation exams word for word – which is already blatant plagiarism. That is why some authorities do not recommend use of a Brain Dump PMP guide.

To be considered passing, your score in the real PMP exam should be at least 106 correct answers out of the 175 scored questions. One disadvantage with this exam is if you leave a certain question blank, this is considered a wrong answer and counted against you.

General Questions on PMP Certification Exam

In passing the Project Management Professional certification, it is essential to have the necessary preparation. PMP certification exam is actually considered as one of the most difficult certification test. To qualify for the test, there are some tips that will help professionals in answering the test questions correctly. Check these lists for general tips:

1. In answering the certification exam question, candidates need to memorize all the necessary formulas such as PERT and Earned Value.
2. This is not a "right minus wrong" type of exam, it is suggested not to leave any test question vacant.
3. To make it safe, each question should be answered based on what PMBOK guide says. Candidates are taking a long shot if they base it on their own experiences.
4. Professionals sometimes encounter questions that they don't even know the answer. In this case, educated guessing is a wise step. This exam has a time limit. Examinees have approximately 80 seconds to finish each test question.
5. If questions are difficult, try to go back later and answer it. In this way examinees will have more time to finish the test.
6. In multiple choice, candidates should put only one answer for every question. In this case, just choose the most relevant statement in the given choices.

The PMP certification exam requires sufficient preparation to be able to qualify for the PMP certification. To do that, professionals and project managers should take PMP practice exam to aid them with the right skills and prepare for the demanding job of project management.

PMP Certification: A Product of PMI

The Project Management Institute or PMI is the one responsible for coming up with the PMP or Project Management certification. It was introduced in 2005 as a means uplifting quality project management procedures which must be implemented among high ranking positions. Upon receipt of a PMP certification, a person automatically possesses a marketable value and a powerful managerial credential.

If you are thinking about acquiring the PMP certification, here are the necessary requirements you must meet.

1. Present your high school diploma to PMI and have it certified

2. You need to meet the specific requirements for educational attainment. This usually means that you should have at least dedicated 35 hours of project management education.

3. You must have incurred work experience in relation to project management. For a span of 8 years, you should have at least participated in work as a project manager for a minimum period of 60 months.

4. A pre-certification exam is given to PMP aspirants to be able to assess the individual's current knowledge in project management. The test is made up of 200 questions in multiple-choice format.

In the event that the person does not pass the exam or was not able to meet all requirements stated above, he or she can opt to get the CAMP, Certified Associate in Project Management, certification instead. However, it is not required that you have the CAMP certificate before you can get the PMP.

However, if the person proceeds on and finally gets a PMP certification, their PMP certification would be granted within a period of three years.

Certification PMP: The Value

For most people, having the Certification is like having the ultimate driving license.

First, it would entail rigorous training and serious concentration much like in learning how to drive.

Second, the process is a long preparation that is meant for the applicants to utilize wisely and not waste.

There are also many tutorial centers, books, driving schools and such; the likes of which, being like in a Certification Examination.

And third, a failure to pass the stringent Examinations of both driving and Certification Examinations would result to basically the same hardship. The value of the Certification Examination is greatly seen on the faces of the people, who have unfortunately failed, and to those people, who have passed. For one, Cindy and Karla were once both applicants, and both failed in passing the Examinations.

This is how important a Certification Examination is. Cindy was not promoted and Alex was never accepted at the company he was applying to. In fact, these are the most likely result of failing in the Examinations.

This is no wonder why more and more applicants are availing themselves the use of PMP tutorial books and PDF review materials. No one wants to fail, and to do so, would ultimately mean dire consequences for all who does fail.

There is another part of this Certification. In the event of a passing, the applicants can now have the right to use the abbreviation of PMP on their name.

This is already quite a plus. In fact, because of this, the mere mention of the name, followed by the PMP, would generally signify already the person's achievement, even without a resume. Now, this Certification is not a magic paper or a miracle-provider. It is just an aid to ensure the user's success.

Why Certifications in CISSP CISA PMP Business Continuity MCSE Security is Important

Today, business organizations are investing heavily on information technology. With millions of dollars at stake, many companies obviously require the services of certified professionals to handle their investment.

With certified professionals, business organizations are assured of the skills and knowledge necessary to maintain their IT equipment and software. Certifications like CISSP, CISA, PMP, Business Continuity, MCSE Security are just some of the few of the many certifications being taken by many individuals today.

Certified Information Systems Security Professional or CISSP is a certification given to individuals who posses the skills and knowledge of various information security topics. The Certified Information Systems Auditor or CISA is primarily concerned with auditing professional certification.

PMP or the Project Management Professional is a world renowned certification in project management. The Microsoft Certified Systems Engineer or MCSE is a part of Microsoft Certified Professional certifications that qualifies individuals as capable of analyzing and implementing IT business solutions.

All certifications point to another important aspect: Business Continuity. Business Continuity is not a certification per se but is a part of disaster recovery which allows an organization to continue functioning even in the event of a disaster.

But getting these certifications is not an easy task. Whether the individual will choose CISSP, CISA, PMP, Business Continuity, MCSE Security, the chances of passing the exam are not that high. The standards of passing these exams are very strict.

As a matter of fact, government institutions like the US Department Of Defense already make it a point to only allow IT certified individuals to handle their IT infrastructure-- such is the importance of having a certificate in CISP, CISA, PMP, Business Continuity, MCSE Security.

Why Would Anyone Sell Discount PMP Books?

PMP stands for the accreditation standards for Project Management – hence it refers to a Project Management Professional (or someone who has attained the desired level of proficiency for that ranking.) Discount PMP books are simply books (or textbooks) to be used for preparing for the PMP accreditation exam – but the books are sold at a discount.

How is it possible to buy discount PMP books then? One way is through bulk purchases. If you have a lot of classmates who are committed to taking the PMP exam at the same time as you are, you might want to ask them to join you in ordering a bulk purchase of the PMP books you need. This actually is considered favorable by publishers who may need to sell off their surplus PMP books to make way for new inventory anyway. It is also beneficial for the PMP examinees as well who can reap cost savings when they join in bulk purchase efforts.

Another way to get discount PMP books is to order straight from the publisher. By using this method, you bypass middlemen like bookstores, wholesalers, and even websites who take a cut from the purchase price of the book to cover their own expenses and profit margins. Some publishers may also offer their own sites (online and in real time) where you can place your order or orders for the discount PMP books. Publishers do this to maintain more control over the distribution of their books and also to help out readers who prefer to buy their books at a much lower cost than that offered by any retail establishments.

Download PMBOK 2000: Use the Safe Ones

The onset of Internet and Websites brought together Information Technology, and this presented numerous, if not many, ways in which persons may exchange ideas easier than in the past.

And the increasing number and for Certifications brought more and more applicants wanting to have a Body of Knowledge for their Examination Certifications.

This is made apparent to any person by use of the Internet Search Engines. But the problem lies with believing the information being provided to the reader. As one Project Manager testifies, he was duped into downloading a Project Manager Body of Knowledge 2000 (PMBOK 2000) for free and all he got was a download-full of Computer viruses.

This person laments that he should have downloaded those that offer PMBOK 2000 for a price. Those that have a fee would usually be the ones who are safe to download, while those that go for free are the ones that must be doubted first.

This is not to discredit the Websites that offer free ones, but in some cases viruses have been known to come from free downloads. And viruses are a menace to any computer, especially on a computer being used by an applicant training for the PMP Certification Examination, who practically needs no disruptions and problems.

The Certification Examination is hard enough without the disruptions. Although there have been free downloads that really offer PMBOK 2000 and not viruses, caution must still be exercised by the user. In the end, the only advise to be given by those, who have been given viruses, is for the future users to determine first before using the safety of the materials to be downloaded.

Tips In Finding Free Downloads In PMP Study Materials

PMP study materials are necessary for passing the exams. Aside from the usual stuff you can buy at various stores and bookshops, free downloads in PMP study materials are also now available online.

There are various websites which are very much accessible and can provide you with these free downloads. Free downloads in PMP study materials are often found in project management websites and even the PMI website would help you in searching for good quality materials.

However, there are some tips you need to remember when looking for free downloads in PMP study materials on various websites.

First, you need to consider the size of the download. Does it really justify how large the space it would eventually take within your hard disk?

You need to be mindful of this so that you can be sure that no other unwanted attachments will be added to your download. This is also necessary so that you can compare the software size with the current ability of your computer.

Aside from the size, free downloads in PMP study materials must also provide you with a sneak peak of what the materials look like. By doing do, you will be able to observe how detailed-oriented it is and how easy it would be for you to understand everything that's inside the materials.

Also, you have to see if the free downloads in PMP study materials also offer you access to online forums. You would find this very beneficial so that you can form networks with other aspirants as well.

Download Free PMP Exam

Being a Project Management Professional, it involves great knowledge in the principles, standards and techniques in project management. In the business industry especially in IT, competition is tight. Professionals should constantly look for ways to enhance their skills in the latest trends in the business. Today, professionals can now avail of free PMP exam online. There are several PMP practice tests in the internet that can make it easier for students to review and evaluate their skills in project management.

Free PMP Exam is a helpful tool that will assist professionals in passing the PMP test. This will provide them with practice test questions that will help them review and prepare for the certification exam. Without continuous trainings it is impossible to keep up with the fast growing market. The PMP exam will test the expertise of professionals in decision making, handling people and the team, and allocate resources in the project.

Apart from that, they will also learn how to make project planning, project initiation, project control, professional responsibility project implementing/execution and project closing. To pass the exam, PMP practice exam is needed to have a comprehensive study on these topics. PMP practice exam also provide the skills, techniques and tools that are utilized in real PMP test.

Aside from that, free PMP exam sites provide tips that can help students and professionals in passing the exam. To make it more convenient for professionals who are working, free online PMP practice exam can be downloaded. All they have to do is have a quick search in the internet for the latest PMP practice exam. By doing so, practitioners, students and professionals will be able to save more money and time in getting training courses.

Free 3rd Edition PMBOK Exam Simulation Book: Practice Question Those Will Help Professionals

Project Management Body of Knowledge PMBOK is considered to be the official guide in project management. This aids professionals in different fields to provide them with proper concepts and standards. Aside from the first version of PMBOK that was released in 1994, several editions of PMBOK followed. The 3rd edition is considered to be the latest edition of PMBOK. There is also free PMBOK Exam Simulation Book that is available online to assist practitioners in passing the certification test.

Project management demands adequate training to successfully implement projects in IT, engineering, construction, automotive and other industries. To do that, project managers need to equip themselves with free practice tests that provide simulation of PMI test question. This will help them in preparing for the certification exam and applying it in the actual job environment. Getting the PMBOK Exam Simulation Book is an effective tool to measure the students' basic comprehension on PMP. This latest edition of the guide will allow the candidate to view their test results and asses what area needs improvement.

Each question on the free PMBOK Exam Simulation Book will give detailed explanations on answers. This will give better comprehension in various concepts of project management. This 200- question test is an integrated exam that includes professional and social responsibility of project managers and practitioners. This also includes the fundamental framework of project management. PMBOK Exam Simulation Book can be downloaded for free online. Just look for the latest version which is the 3rd edition. Downloading this will surely help professionals in passing requirements for PMP certification.

A Quick View on History of PMBOK

The Project Management Body of Knowledge(PMBOK) is viewed as the official guide for project management. This document is the crucial foundation to successfully pass the PMP certification test.

The history of PMBOK started with a small group in 1968. J. Gordon Davis, Edward A. Engman, Eric Jenett and James R. Snyder initiated the formation of this organization. These men are completely committed and dedicated to enhance and develop the discipline of project management. Later on, Susan C. Gallagher joined others.

Soon after, they named the organization as Project Management Institute (PMI). The history of PMI is an encouraging testimony to other non profit organizations in the business industry.

This group rapidly grew as a huge association with over 250,000 professional members all over the world.

In 1986, PMI created a guide which is called Project Management Body of Knowledge. This innovative document helps project managers and professionals in their providing them with strategic plans, methods, standards and concepts in project management.

Not long after, the PMBOK became an official guide and ANSI standard. There are several editions that were published. In 1994, the very first edition of PMBOK was published in the market. After that, the revised version was released in 1996.

In 1999, PMBOK 2000 was established and later on the third edition was made public in year 2004. Indeed, the history of

PMBOK will continuously move forward as the demand for better processes in project management increase. PMBOK will also constantly develop to meet the demands of the business industry.

A Backgrounder on the PMBOK Form of Accreditation

The first ever Project Management Body of Knowledge Guide (or PMBOK) was published by the organization called the PMI (or Project Management Institute) in the year 1987 as an attempt to standardize and document generally accepted project management practices and information. The most up-to-date edition is entitled Guide to the Project Management Body of Knowledge, third edition (also called the PMBOK guide for short.) The book was released on October 31 of year 2004 and proved to be useful as a basic guide for Project Management.

The third edition PMBOK Guide is also recognized as the international standard for Project Management recognized all over the world (IEEE Std 1490-2003). The PMBOK guide provides the essentials in Project Management by discussing a wide variety of projects (including software, construction, automotive, and engineering, among others.) The PMBOK Guide works by helping project processes be identified (hence PMBOK can be said to be a Process-based guide.) The book is also consistent with a variety of other management standards like the Software Engineering Institute CMMI and ISO 9000. Since processes interact and overlap through various phases of a project, processes are explained in terms of: Tools and Techniques, Inputs, and Outputs.

The PMBOK Guide discusses the Process Groups and different Areas of Management. The five divisions of process groups are called Initiating, Planning, Executing, Monitoring and Controlling, and Closing.

The nine Knowledge Areas in Management are deemed to be Project Integration Management, Project Time Management,

Project Scope Management, Project Quality Management, Project Cost Management, Project Communications Management, Project Human Resource Management, Project Procurement Management and Project Risk Management.

PMBOK may teach a practitioner what to do in a project, but will not automatically teach the how to part. The main purpose of the PMBOK is to guide practitioners via experience so they can achieve knowledge on how to run an IT Project or other types of projects.

PMBOK Sample Document: A Quick View on Project Management Concepts

The Project Management Body of Knowledge or PMBOK is a compilation of best practices, procedures and processes in project management. This official document helps professionals in managing the different discipline in project management. This gives a fundamental knowledge in handling projects in different areas such as software, IT, the engineering, construction, automotive and other fields in the business industry. A sample document of PMBOK is easily accessible in the internet to provide professionals the fundamental knowledge in project management.

The PMBOK is a useful tool that helps project managers to effectively implement the basic standards, techniques and principles in their projects. Reviewing a sample of PMBOK together with PMP trainings and practice tests will ensure an individual's qualification for PMP certification. This will help students in studying the different methods of implementing projects.

PMBOK has various editions. PMI ensures that the concepts and principles in project management are updated to provide students and professionals the latest techniques in initiating, planning, executing, monitoring and controlling the various processes in project management. When downloading sample document, make sure to use the 3rd edition of PMBOK. This document will help improve the project management processes in today's business environment.

To have a successful career in project management, it is essential to have the necessary skills and credentials. Companies these days search for not just skilled professionals but they are also looking for people who gained certifications in project management. Making use of free sample of PMBOK document online can help practitioners in preparing for the PMP certification test.

The Significance of Downloading a PMBOK Guide

Before anyone could be Project Management Professional, it is initially important to pass the certification exam. To pass this test, professionals, project managers and students need to be equipped with tools that can help them prepare for the big test. Project management is a difficult and comprehensive test that requires guidance form the official PMBOK guide.

The Project Management Body of Knowledge Guide (PMBOK) is considered as an important tool to review and pass the certification exam.

Today, this guide can now be easily downloaded online. This actually helps professionals, practitioners and students in providing them the necessary skills and knowledge in project management. Interested individuals can download the PMBOK in eight different languages.

In this guide there are about nine knowledge areas that have all the processes needed to accomplish a successful management program. These are:
1. Project Quality Management
2. Project Cost Management
3. Project Integration Management
4. Project Scope Management
5. Project Procurement Management
6. Project Risk Management
7. Project Time Management
8. Project Human Resource Management
9. Project Communications Management

There are several sites in the internet that can help candidates the download PMBOK Guides. Some offer it for free, while some ask for a minimal fee to download the whole guide.

This will definitely help project managers all over the world. This will allow examinees to study the book and take the exam in their preferred language. It actually took PMI a year to comprehensively translate the guide to several languages. Now candidates can avail and download the PMBOK in their chosen language.

Free PMBOK Guide for Professionals

The Project Management Body of Knowledge Guide (PMBOK) is regarded as the official book for project management. This is used as a fundamental basis for the certification test. This book documents the different practices, standards and methods used in managing projects in software, construction, automotive, engineering, IT and many more. Free downloads in the internet are available to make it more accessible to students who wish to study the document.

To get a certification in project management it is necessary to review the PMBOK guide. Without studying this document, it will be very difficult to successfully pass the Project Management Professional certification. Free PMBOK guide can help professionals, practitioners and project managers to know the basic processes in project management. These processes include Tools and Techniques (mechanisms applied to inputs), Output (consists of documents, products, services and many more), Inputs (design, construction, documents and plans)

Although this guide is considered as the major source of principles, methods and concepts, PMBOK does not claim that all techniques and methods are applicable in all project cases. Deciding what is best for a certain case is the primary responsibility of project managers and core group. To effectively utilize this document and pass the certification test, professionals should make use of free training courses and practice tests. All these can be downloaded for free. Just look for recent versions to efficiently utilize the document and ensure a successful qualification to PMP certification exam. Getting a PMBOK guide plays a great part in passing the test. So avail this document online while it's free.

PMBOK Free Download: Mixed Concerns

In the onset of Internet Access and Websites, there exist a way in which sharing information was made easy. This information is readily available to all those with computers and Internet Access. Today even children are given computer lessons at school.

In the Certification Examinations, there are already many downloadable materials that offer for a fee. There are also some that offer their materials for free of price. The funny thing is that there are people, who claim as to have been helped by these free downloadable PMBOK.

They even swear that it helped them a lot with the Examinations and that they passed. On the other hand, there are also numerous occasions, all coming from people, who have been disgruntled by how the free downloadable PMBOK were portrayed to help but did not.

Some even claimed to had been sent viruses, instead of the PMBOK. But what matters most is that the people, who mean to download the materials should do well to inquire first of the safety of the product they are about to get.

This is not to say that all free downloadable PMBOK's are worthless or even dangerous. Some are, but this should not stop people from trying them out. After all, they are for free. In the term, mixed concerns, the users of the data should be able discern whether they should try to take the risk of using a free one in lieu of the one that comes with a price tag. It is simply within the users' responsibilities.

What is a PMBOK Guide

The Project Management Body of Knowledge is an important guide to successfully pass the Project Management certification. It is essential to help interested professionals in enhancing their skills and providing them the concepts and standards of project management. This includes the best practices and innovative methods to manage the projects.

The PMBOK guide is the official book that provides the candidates a fundamental reference. This guide cannot be considered to have all the comprehensive data needed in project management. The PMBOK generally have the applicable and appropriate practices in the industry. On the other hand, this does not mean that these practices are consistently applied in each case. It is the responsibility of the project management team to decide on the appropriate assessment to the project.

The PMBOK guide acts as the official source for anyone who wish to have a career in project management. This guide also gives a comprehensive understanding on the basic structures of project management.

This document has nine different Project Management Knowledge Areas such as Project Risk Management, Project Integration Management, Project Time Management, Project Cost Management, Project Quality Management, Project Communications Management, Project Procurement Management, Project Human Resource Management and Project Scope Management.

The International Organization for Standardization actually worked with PMI to create the PMBOK guide. They also seek feedback from the project management experts and representatives around the world to help improve and enhance the concepts, practices and processes of the PMBOK guide. This will help project managers, practitioners and students in updating their skills to cope with the progressing standards in the business industry.

What is PMBOK PDF

The Project Management Professional is one of the most comprehensive certifications available in the business industry. This will help practitioners, students and project managers in the development of their skills in project management.

This certification needs an extensive preparation to pass PMP exam. To meet this goal, there are tools such as pdf files and ebooks that can help professionals and practitioners. The Project Management Body of Knowledge or PMBOK is the official book recommended by PMI to aid students in their study.

Aside from that, this is PMI's basis in creating the Project Management Professional certification exam. The PMP certification is one of the most difficult certification exams.

That is why professionals must train themselves to be able to qualify for this certification. This guide will give them the advantage in obtaining the latest concepts, standards and techniques in project management.

The PMBOK pdf has 44 fundamental processes that fall under the 9 knowledge areas and 5 process groups of project management.

The 9 knowledge areas are the following:
* Project Communications Management
* Project Time Management
* Project Integration Management
* Project Human Resource Management
* Project Scope Management
* Project Cost Management
* Project Procurement Management
* Project Quality Management

*   Project Risk Management 5 process groups:
*   Initiating,
*   Planning,
*   Executing,
*   Controlling and Monitoring, and
*   Closing The PMBOK

pdf can be downloaded in several sites online. Some are free and some offer it with a minimal fee. To ensure the success in getting the certification, download the latest documents of PMBOK pdf.

What is PMI and PMBOK Project Management Institute

PMI is non-profit organization that is considered to be the leading association for project management. PMI was actually founded in 1969 by five professionals who wanted to create an impact in networking, give solution to the project problems and share concepts and information processes in project management. PMI is actively pursuing the advocacy in this field.

They are known to perform research to improve the standards in project management. Aside from that PMI also supports other activities such as professional development and certification. They also play a vital role in offering networking, communications and community opportunities. PMI also instigated the development of Project Management Body of Knowledge or PMBOK.

This guide is considered to be the basic foundation of Project Management certification exam. This document provides the basic reference for the PMP test. The PMBOK guide was first released in 1987 to create a standard in project management and provide students the essential concepts on practices.

This enables professionals, project managers and practitioners review the five process groups such as Initiating, Planning, Executing, Controlling and Monitoring, and Closing. To have an effective project management program, it is also important for companies to implement the nine knowledge areas stated in PMI's PMBOK Guide.

These are Project Procurement Management, Project Time Management, Project Quality Management, Project Human Resource Management, Project Communications Management,

Project Scope Management, Project Risk Management, Project Integration Management and Project Cost Management. To date, these processes and concepts are actively used by project managers to successfully implement an effective project management.

What are the Components of the PMBOK Process?

The Project Management Body of Knowledge (or PMBOK) is a set of best practices of Project Management, broken down into different processes and areas of knowledge in this field of discipline. The PMBOK is classified as the IEEE Std 1490-2003 standard of Project Management concepts that can be applied in multiple types of occupation.

The five main process groups may overlap and work in synergy within a certain phase or for the project it self. You can define a process based on its inputs (such as the design, plan, or documents used); mechanism used for inputs (like techniques and tools employed); and outputs employed (namely the products and documents that come into play.)

The nine areas of knowledge may be composed of at least one of the five main process groups (or a combination of two or more.)

You may find that majority of the PMBOK database is especially applicable to Project Management alone. The PMBOK is a special product of the Project Management Institute.

The Project Management Institute may allow you to take the first level of Project Management certification which is the Certified Associate in Project Management (or CAPM) form of accreditation. Or you could aim directly for the Project Management Professional certification (or PMP.)

If you opt for the first level of certification, that means you have pursued at least 1500 hours of work within project team conditions; or that you have completed academic training in Project Management reaching up to 23 contact hours.

For the second level, you need to prove you have been pursuing continuous experience and education in Project Management before three years are up or you forfeit your PMP ranking.

What is the value Project Management Institute's PMP Certification?

There is value in the PMP only for a few, narrow purposes:
1. To gain credibility and salary, IF you are in the information systems area or happen to work for an employer or client that values the PMP greatly
2. To learn the PMBOK language and terms, so you can communicate better with other PMPs
3. To help break into the Project Management Institute community, perhaps as a volunteer, speaker, or author

The PMP is genuinely useful in helping project managers from different industries and countries to talk to each other. Whether one person talks about "critical path" or "soft dependencies" or "discretionary logic" depends on their industry. Having a common language helps us all talk together. The PMBOK Guide and PMP have provided a common vocabulary for project managers, and that is its greatest achievement.

It is also valuable to have a PMP if you want to become active within PMI. Some volunteers who have had years of experience do not get it. The most senior people are unofficially "grandfathered" by their reputation. Anyone new is usually going to have their PMP. It is not a rule, but it is common practice.

Regarding getting an MBA vs. a PMP, the two are very different. An MBA is an intense, one-time event. A PMP is an on-going certification and continuing education program. Depending on the job, one will be more valuable than the other. It depends on the role and the job.

PMI Leading the way to Project Management Professional Certification

The Project Management Institute (PMI) is well known non-profit organization who initiated the project management certification. This association has achieved a lot in several advocacy programs related to project management. They have supported different agencies in the government, industries and organizations all throughout the world to help them attain great business outcomes.

This organization is also initiated the Project Management Professional (PMP) certification to help professionals advance their skills in handling projects in engineering, construction, software, automotive, and many more.

In 1987, PMI started to publish the Project Management Body of Knowledge or PMBOK that documents best practices, concepts and techniques. This guide is necessary to prepare and study for the PMP certification.

PMP is certification that is necessary to boost a professionals' resume. This will help them gain a prestigious certification that can provide them a better career in project management. However before anyone can get PMP certification is essential to pass PMP exam. This test is a comprehensive exam that measures the skills and knowledge of project managers, professionals and practitioners.

PMI together with other experts in project management, continuously update and improve the PMP exam and PMBOK guide to help professionals gain all the needed knowledge in project management.

PMI is an established organization and has earned several prestigious awards. This includes the award given by International Organization for Standardization (ISO) which the "ISO/IEC 17024 accreditation for the Project Management Professional (PMP®) credential program." This has given PMI a great leverage to be most acknowledged certification program in the project management.

Why Should I Pursue PMI PMP Certification?

PMI stands for Project Management Institute while PMP certification is the accreditation in Project Management Professional administered by the PMI. The advantage with being accredited by PMI in PMP certification is that the PMI system adheres to ISO 9001 certification in Quality Management Systems. PMI is also globally recognized so if you get your PMI PMP certification you know your employer (wherever he might be or wherever you might be destined) will accept your certification results.

The PMP certification itself has already been granted ISO 17024 accreditation as well. This is good because existing accredited PMPs (or Project Management Professionals) will be deemed accredited as well. Another benefit is that the new ISO 17024 accreditation will allow employees to be deemed competent based on this quality standards. Any future candidates for PMP certification will also gain global acceptance among their PMP peers and the industry itself.

To allow the PMP certification to stay upgraded, you have to participate in the CCR (or Continuing Certification Requirements) program. If you do not keep your PMP certification upgraded, you essentially forfeit your PMP certification.

One reason you ought to sustain the status of your PMP certification is that it is one way for you to stay competitive in the current job market. If you sustain PMP certification, it means you are staying proficient in the Project Management Body of Knowledge (or PMBOK) which is the basis for accreditation in Project Management in the first place. And this assures PMI that its own system is being followed by all who claim to have PMP status.

The Importance of PMI and PMP Preparation Course

PMI designed a certification that provides professionals a chance to enhance their skills and give their career an open door to new opportunities. The Project Management Professional (PMP) is one of the requirements to get a job in project management. Especially for project managers, it is important to have the essential certifications to successfully compete with other candidates in the job market. This will give them leverage in leading the projects and it will provide them with the confidence they need to effectively implement the tasks with the team.

The PMI initiated a prestigious certification that needs proper preparation and comprehensive training. There are preparation courses that can help professionals and practitioners to qualify for the test. These courses aim to provide the candidates to efficiently plan and study the different requirements of PMP exam. This includes intensive training in standards, concepts, methods and techniques in project management.

The preparation course also includes learning materials to help candidates practice and review for the intensive PMP test. The materials include workbooks where professionals can answer anytime. There are also audio CDs to provide a thorough application of skills and knowledge in project management. In addition to that, PMP exam simulator software, poster illustrations and instructional DVDs are also included if candidates avail of preparation course. Interested candidates can just browse in the internet for sites that offer this course. This PMP preparation course will definitely help participants in gaining the knowledge in exam topics and this will provide tips in the exam preparation.

What is the PMP Certification issued by the Project Management Institute?

When we talk about PMP, we may be referring to the project management certification granted exclusively by the Project Management Institute. This form of accreditation awards the recipient the status of Project Management Professional. To receive the PMP certification, you need to take and pass an exam first, which is based on the PMBOK Guide (also called A Guide to the Project Management Body of Knowledge) which is produced by the Project Management Institute itself.

Actually, the Project Management Institute awards certification based on a three-step ladder. At the very first rung would be the Certified Associate in Project Management (or CAPM) which project team members are meant to aim for. The second rung in this ladder is the PMP Certification and is deemed the standard by which all PM certifications should be measured against. After being granted true PMP Certification, the individual is permitted to use the initials PMP after his name. The third rung (called the Program Management Professional certification) is meant for Program Managers and was only offered to the public this 2007.

To qualify for the PMP exam itself, the candidate can present his high school diploma, an ethical code of conduct for professionals, and the accreditation exam itself (which should gauge the comprehensive knowledge of the candidate in the field of Project Management.)

The PMP accreditation needs to be updated via continuing professional education and training; otherwise, the PMP himself will forfeit his PMP accreditation.

What to Expect at PMP Boot Camp

Project Management Professional (PMP) certification is considered as one of the most sought after certifications in the field of construction, engineering, automotive, IT, software and many more. Getting a PMP certification is a wise investment on a professional's credential. In addition to that, it will also boost a practitioner's resume. This will definitely help in getting a head start in the different processes and procedures in project management. Enrolling on PMP boot camp is one of the options in getting good training in project management. This will absolutely help students and project managers to effectively apply the processes in PMP.

The PMP certification exam requires having an intensive training and hands on experience. This 5 day PMP boot camp is a comprehensive training course that uses supports PMI's Project Management Body of Knowledge (PMBOK) guide. PMP boot camp will help candidates and project managers to focus on the intensive training of experts in project management. This training will assist professionals in gaining the processes and knowledge areas in project management. Aside from that, PMP boot camp enables practitioners to successfully implement PMP projects.

The PMP boot camp allows students to have a solid foundation in project management. In this training, best practices, concepts and principles of project management are given emphasis. Aside from that, this course is established to provide the required skills needed in PMP planning, PMP tracking concepts and focus on strategic approach on managing people in the team. This training alternative is one of the best ways to enhance the skills of professionals in project management.

A Short Definition of the PMP Certification

The PMP Certification is considered the second-highest form of Project Management accreditation there is which is administered by the Project Management Institute. Once you have earned the PMP Certification, you are allowed to use it for three years afterwards. But a PMP (the title for someone who has earned PMP Certification) is required to use these three years to earn his Professional Development Units (or PDUs) to prove continual efforts at professional development.

The field of Project Management itself is a field of discipline that allows the manager to undertake management of various resources of a project within the bounds of the cost, time, quality and scope of the project itself. It should be stressed that a project is always a temporary sustained effort over a period of time. Project Management had its origins in the fields of defense, engineering, and construction.

If the applicant for PMP Certification cannot present a high school diploma when applying for the PMP accreditation exam, it is possible to present a document showing an equivalent form of academic attainment too to qualify. Other requirements sought after in a PMP accreditation candidate are: to have worked as a task manager in some project for at least 7,500 hours, have worked as a Project Manager for a minimum of 60 months in the last eight years, and have earned at least 35 hours of Project Management academic training under his belt with emphasis on PMI methodologies. If you have already earned your bachelor's degree, you can then undertake only a minimum of 4,500 hours of work as a task manager in a project, and present proof of experience lasting at least 36 months to qualify.

Tips on Taking the PMP Certification Exam

The Project Management Certification Exam is an essential test that needs adequate preparation and training. Without the help of PMBOK and other PMP trainings it will be difficult for professionals to pass this certification exam. In this test, professionals must be able to know the concepts, keep on practicing exam questions and get training courses to ensure that they pass the test.

To help professionals get started, here are some tips that can help them qualify for the PMP certification:

*   To pass the PMP certification exam, professionals should not base it on their perspective or experiences from the job. Instead, it is necessary to think from PMI's point of view. People have different job experiences; that is why it is not wise to base the exam answers on it. *   In answering the PMP exam, practitioners should be cautious on choosing answers that use generalizations. Using always, must, never, etc. are most of the time wrong answers. *   Using sometimes, often, generally, may and perhaps are acceptable answers for special cases. *   There are trick questions in PMP exam. There are actually questions that have additional information on it. This is created to confuse and test the comprehension of the candidate. Be cautious on this extra information because not all of it are necessary to answer the question.

It is essential to have a PMP certification especially project managers who want to have higher salary. These tips in certification exam will certainly help them in passing the PMP test and provide professionals with greater opportunities in the future.

The Importance of PMP Certification Training

Project Management Professional or PMP is a well known certification that gives great opportunities in project management. The Project Management Institute initiated this examination to enhance the skills and knowledge of professionals. This program offers an advanced concepts and knowledge in Project Management. It is also considered as one of the most difficult certification and training that is available.

The PMP training is rigorous process. It requires a serious training and can cost you a lot. However, the PMP certification training is primarily a good investment for skills. This will surely help professionals increase their salary and aim to get a promotion. Good thing there are training centers and internet sites that will aid students in passing the certification test. To make it more convenient for IT professionals, there are PMP certification trainings that are available online. This can help interested individuals in getting the right trainings without leaving their office.

As a professional, it is hard to leave the office just to attend classroom based trainings. Aside from that, candidates can take trainings anytime of the day. Some sites online offer test prep and study guides that can help professionals in successfully acquiring their certification. These are essential things to get before deciding to take the PMP test. Project management offers a very demanding job. Practitioners and students alike must be able to enhance their skills and knowledge in order to effectively compete with other professionals in the industry. The PMP certification training will surely help candidates in equipping them with the right skills in project management.

Choose the Right PMP Training Course

Obtaining the PMP is not an easy thing to do. Preparations are very much necessary to ensure that the person would not end up wasting all of his efforts just to get that certification. This is why training courses are a must. PMP courses which are geared towards PMP training helps equip the individual with necessary knowledge to get that coveted certificate.

Since there are a lot of PMP courses offering efficient prep-up methods prior to the exam day, here's a list of useful tips you should look at before zeroing in on the best choice.

1. Look at the course's strategy when it comes to test-taking. A good PMP training course should let you on basic exam know-hows.

2. The course should also have a focus on important project management activities such diagramming networks, forward and backward pass, to name a few. Chances are, you would come across these topics during the exam.

3. There should be an online course easily accessible for people who wish to avail of the program. The online course must have an easily accessible class discussion forum and a PMP coach who would facilitate online course discussion. This online site must be accessible 24/7 without limits.

4. PMP Training courses approved by the PMI should also be verified. It would be wise to look at the PMI website for more details regarding affiliates. A PMI approval means that the course closely follows PMI standards when it comes to PMP certification, which is why training courses would aim to be approved by the PMI.

Why Project Managers Need to Take PMP Training Courses

Project managers today need to have various skills to perform the demanding tasks in project management. Monitoring, planning, initiating and implementing huge scale projects are just some of the major responsibilities of a project manager. They need to learn how to multi-task and use strategies appropriate for the project. In this case, PMP training courses can help professionals get all the necessary skills and knowledge to equip them. Training courses will professionalize the job experience of project managers in their field.

There are different requirements for every PMP program. There are courses that require candidates to have at least five years of job experience. Some training courses does not need perquisites in order to sign up. In PMP training courses, it formalizes the experience of professionals. Also, this credential can take them to greater heights in their career. That is why it is crucial to take courses in order to enhance the managerial skills and technical expertise of project managers. The PMP courses basically include topics on communications, risk management, time and cost management, project procurement abilities and many more. Furthermore, the skills acquired in this course can be applied in real job environment.

To make it more convenient for project managers and professionals, online courses are now available to fit their lifestyle and hectic schedule. Professionals can choose from various options. Audio/ video CD, pdf files and training software are some of the alternatives in getting online trainings. In this generation, everything can be accessed in the internet. Taking online courses is one of the most convenient and worry-free methods of advancing the abilities of professionals.

How to Qualify for the PMP Exam

The variations on the PMP acronym meaning may refer to many things. Some of them may stand for Point to Multipoint Communication (PMP in Telecommunications), NAT Port Mapping Protocol, Permanent Monitoring Panel, Perlman Music Program, Project Management Plan (which is also part of Project Management), Portable Media Player (which involves the areas of Image, Audio, Video, DMB, e-book devices and, Automotive Navigation System), Protected Media Path, and Project Management Professional (Certification for Project Management Professionals) – among many others.

But for our purposes, the PMP in Project Management can be narrowed down to mean just Project Management Plan and Project Management Professional (which are both included in the definition of Project Management.)

A Project Management Plan normally discusses project execution systems that are included in the main aspects of project management. These could be Schedule Management, Scope Management, Financial Management, Resource Management for human resources (which may mean tools among other things), Quality Management, Project Change Management, Communication Management, Procurement Management, and Risk Management. The Project Management Plan is usually required by professional Project Management firms and other large companies to ensure that the standard version of the Project Management plan is approved in the early phases of the project and continues to be implemented until the end of the project.

The other meaning of PMP could be Project Management Professional. It is a globally recognized form of certification in Project Management. The PMP form of accreditation is managed by the PMI or Project Management Institute. It is based on the PMO Examination Specification which was made by PMI in year 2005.

You stand to receive the PMP Certificate if you succeed in passing an examination administered by the PMI. The first step is to schedule an examination at any of the Prometric testing centers. Examination is in multiple choice format, and you may choose your examination time from a schedule that also includes weekends and after working hours. Examinees are expected to complete the test made up of 200 questions (with dummy questions) in 4 hours with a minimal success rate of 60.5%.

PMP Examination: The Second Tier Examination

In the Certification Examination for the PMP the candidate will have to go through a series of questions for him to answer correctly and substantially. Alex an applicant for the Certification Examination once said that it is a very complex Certification. It is noteworthy to state that the PMP Examination is not industry specific, but it is one of the trickiest examinations ever devised. Part of the Examination contains questions with irrelevant information, all of which are meant to confuse the applicant. Also, in this Examination, a question only has one correct answer, and again, the PMI has included many other answers that may appear to be correct, but are highly irrelevant to the whole question. The answering of questions should also be taken into context because the questions are only answerable from a PMI's perspective. Future applicants should be wary of using their own experiences to solve these questions. In the end, they often fail, but one sure-fire way in answering correctly is to answer in a textbook manner. Now, there is no such need for future applicants to be like Alex, who dismally failed in the examinations. There are of course many Internet Websites out there, who are offering tips and trivia about the PMP Examinations. Now, an examinee's application must first be approved by the PMI. After which, he may then have a schedule of Examination on the PMI-approved Examination centers. There is a wide variety of time are available for the examinees. The Examination is also held even during the weekends and after normal working hours. So this great time flexibility can lessen the burden for the applicants.

The Benefits of PMP Exam Prep

The PMP Exam Prep E-book provides an efficient study guide for Project Management. This tool can give students and professionals the comprehensive knowledge in the latest concepts and standards in implementing the proper project management. Aside from that the PMP Exam Prep helps practitioners in passing the certification exam. This includes not just all the things needed in order to pass the test but this also provides the skills professionals can use in their actual job. Exam prep is an effective tool that can also aid the project managers in developing their skills in creating strategies in project management.

The PMP Exam Prep is in line with the PMBOK guide. It has all the basic concepts, exercises and skills needed in order to pass the PMP exam. This also includes exam tips that will surely help in preparing for the test. Exam prep follows organized steps and program study by applying the materials given. Some sites in the internet offer exam prep online. It can be easily be downloaded with a minimal free. There are also free downloadable exam prep online but professionals need to be cautious on downloading old versions.

The Project Management Professional certification can help practitioners, students and young professionals in fulfilling their dream job in project management. By getting a certification, professional can get higher salaries and even acquire a promotion. To pass this certification, interested professionals need to get a PMP Exam Prep to aid them with the right skills. This will help them enhance their knowledge in the certification exam in PMP and PMI.

PMP Exam Prep 4th Edition: The Book for PMP Certification Examination

This is the perfect book for all those applicants wanting to pass the PMP Certification Examinations. In fact, this book is a great help to those, who lack the necessary computer to study PMP with the use of the PDF. It is also a good reading to begin with. There are some people, like in the case of Ms. Corpuz, who can study better with the use of a book than on the Computer Monitor or printout. A book is even handier than a computer simply because a book could be carried anywhere one goes, unlike a Computer, which is obviously bulkier and more to prone breakdowns. It is simply better to have both PDF versions of the PMP and the book on Examination handy when reviewing and taking the Certification Examinations. The Examination is already hard enough without the reading the book, so there would be no excuse into not buying one. Ms. Corpus has even gone into great lengths as to say that without the book, she would not have passed the Certification Examination at all. Inside the book is all the information required by the reader to know all about the PMP Examinations. There are also other parts of the book that are noteworthy. It also includes a review material and practical examinations for the applicants to do mock Examinations. Detailed explanations and insider tips on how questions on the certification Examination would look like and exercises. There are also various games that are programmed to increase the applicant's ability to mettle in dealing with the Examination.

The Basics of PMP Exam Preparation

The PMP exam lasts an average of four hours. You can just imagine how much pressure you have to endure just to bag that PMP certification. Actually, there's no need to worry. All you have to do is come up with the right methods on PMP exam preparation.

There are actually lots of PMP exam preparation courses and classes which are already available. These classes aim to prepare you and give you an idea regarding what you can most probably expect from the actual exam. These courses also help guide you with all the vital information you will need to be able to answer all questions.

These courses and classes are also available online. So no matter where you are and what time you are available, you can actually enroll yourself into one. Classes and courses fit themselves into your schedule so that you won't have to fret about organizing things.

However, if you choose to self-study there are also a lot of good ways you can adapt for PMP exam preparation. There are a lot of books and PMP materials now available in stores for those who want to self-study or pace their own preparation. This method also helps you flexibly speed up or slow down the preparation process without having to worry about anybody else.

Of course, practice exams are also valuable. This is definitely one good method of PMP exam preparation. Practice exams help simulate the actual day and help you evaluate your current capacity to take the certification exam. This method also helps you see your current strengths and weaknesses in test-taking especially for long exams.

The Advantages of PMP Exam Preparation Test

The Project Management Professional (PMP) certification is an essential part of a project manager's resume. This will provide them with vast career opportunities and it will give them more confidence in handling the complex projects in the future. Because of PMP's required rigorous training, professionals will gain not just a impressive resume but also this will provide them with the knowledge and skills needed in the actual job environment. To prepare for the certification test, it is necessary to get exam preparation test to asses and practice for the certification exam.

The PMP exam preparation test is a very important tool that will help practitioners and professionals. This will provide them with an effective exam simulator that will help them in acquiring the Project Management Professional certification. The exam preparation test contains over 850 questions and mock tests that will ensure the candidate's qualification for the PMP certification. There is also practice test software that can help candidates practice and review anytime. This is a convenient way to study even while working in the office.

Most professionals have a hard time preparing for the test because of the demanding work load in project management. It is usually inconvenient for them take classroom based trainings because of the erratic schedule project managers have. Good thing there are exam preparation test that can be downloaded online. Some sites in the internet have money back guarantee on simulated tests and practice exams. Downloading and using exam preparation tests can ensure a professional's qualification for the PMP certification.

What to Expect on PMP Exam Questions

Project Management Professional is one of the most sought after certifications in the business industry. This provides professionals great opportunities in advancing their knowledge and skills in project management. Getting PMP practice test and study guides are also important to pass the certification test. This will help professionals and students in preparing for the actual PMP test. Aside from that, this will enhance their skills that are needed in their actual job environment.

There are certain requirements before candidates can qualify. To acquire the Project Management Professional certification, professionals must be able to pass the required examination in project management. The questions in this test have psychometrically examined. This also has a project management reference and it is approved to comply with the requirements of the project management job. The examination has 200 multiple- choice questions.

The pretest questions consist of 25 items. The test questions consists of 27% executing, 11% initiating, 23% planning, 21% monitoring and controlling, 9% closing, 9% social responsibility and professional. The PMP exam questions must be finished in 4 hours. Some of the requirements include an identification that is issued by the government. If the candidate wishes to take the computer based exam, they can have a copy of the score right after the exam.

To successfully answer all the PMP exam questions, it is essential to get a hold of PMP practice exam and study guides. This will aid the candidates to effectively prepare for the comprehensive examination. Just download the study guide programs online and practice it regularly to qualify for the PMP certification.

PMP Exams: A Great Deal of Convenience and Hard Questions

There are currently many kinds of Certification Examinations being provided by the Programming Companies for users of their programs. In this case, the PMI gives the opportunity for Project managers and employers to test their employees of their skill in Project management.

As seen in the case of Alfred, who had just passed the PMP Certification Examinations, his employer wanted to see if he was experienced enough for promotion. The passing of the PMP was crucial to his success. From being a part of the Project Management team, he is now the Project Manager.

The Examination is far from simple as many others, who have taken it, would attest. It is set in a Multiplication Choice test, but being that, it is still a tad more difficult to pass that the others. It has a series of irrelevant information, which are meant only to confuse the applicant from answering incorrectly. But the good thing about the PMP Certification Examination is its apparent time flexibility in terms of when an applicant may take it.

It is also flexible in terms of where. An applicant, like in the case of Alfred, may choose to take the Examination of the computer. Or, it may be taken in its written form. This makes it a highly convenient Examination to take.

But whatever its conveniences, the Examinees would still have to go through and answer 200 questions in 4 hours.

There are however, 25 trial questions that are not counted as part of the final score. And these are intended as dummy questions, which the examinees have no knowledge about. For a pass to be made, there must be a relative success rate of at least 60.5%.

What is the Value of a PMP Free Test?

The field of Project Management is quite broadly applied to a host of other disciplines, but due to the all-encompassing nature of Project Management there should not be much confusion as to how Project Management can be fused with these other occupations to create unique applications.

To qualify to become a PMP (or Project Management Professional), you need to take a specific exam administered by the Project Management Institute (or PMI.) And to prepare adequately for this exam, you might find a PMP free test to be quite useful.

One type of PMP free test you could undertake could be made up of flash cards – with one card representing one question that most likely would appear on the PMP accreditation exam. The flash card technique has been used by educators for decades (and if you remember your primary school days, you probably used flash cards then as well.)

Another way to get a PMP free test is to go through an online test. Many of these online training courses will allow you access to free tests after the training is culminated. It actually benefits the training provider as well, because if students become better prepared and do get passing or even very high marks on the PMP accreditation exam, that means the reputation of the training provider will be polished even more.

To know if the PMP free test you are eyeing is the right preparation tool for you, check if it covers the areas of Initiation, Planning, Executing, Monitoring and Controlling, Closing, and lastly Professional and Social Responsibility. These are the areas from where the actual exam questions will be sourced.

Applying PMP Human Resources Management Presentation in the Company

Companies nowadays are recognizing the importance of following Project Management and having a Project Management Professional handle Human Resources Management in the presentation of projects. A PMP Human Resources Management presentation assures companies that the individual handling company projects have the necessary skills and knowledge in implementing Project Management principles in the organization.

Having a PMP Human Resources Management presentation adds value to the company's initiative of improving the Human Resources Management because it aids companies in the getting started with project management in their organization.

It has often been regarded that planning, research, communication and review are essential elements in project management and yet these same elements usually laid aside in a rush or time constrained project. But with a PMP Human Resources Management presentation, this mentality of doing projects in a non-cost effective way will be replaced with a successful implementation of projects that are on time, within budget and within the standards of everyone involved.

A PMP Human Resources Management presentation uses a tool or methodology that applies the best practices, procedures and rules used by every successful company. The PMP Human Resources Management presentation adds value to the Human Resources Management because it carefully studies the feasibility of a project and then conducts a cost and benefit analysis before setting expectations on the desired result. This defines the goals of the project and will eventually set an outline on the steps needed to achieve the goals set.

After the initial planning, a PMP Human Resources Management presentation will also apply tracking, and follow-through in every project undertaking to make sure that it meets the standards of the company.

PMP Management Products with Exam and Project Training from RMC

A Project Management Professional is someone who has been certified by the Project Management Institute as capable in implementing Project Management in an organization. The certification is a globally recognized credential and is an excellent addition in the advancement of an individual's career. There are many PMP management products with an exam on project training given by RMC and other online stores or IT bookstores.

RMC Project Management is a training material for the project management exam certification. It focuses on getting the reviewer a PMP certification through its different products on project management. They have preparation books that contain real-world situations on project management. RMC also has computer basted training CDs on exam preparations for PMP certification. Most RMC PMP Management Products have exam flash cards that help you in project training. This way, the individual can practice wherever and whenever he feels like it.

Getting PMP Management products with an exam on project training from RMC has many great advantages. With RMC PMP training products an individual's development and training are easily developed because the course material can be easily updated and the CDs, books, and flash cards can be easily brought anywhere and anytime.

PMP Management products from RMC provide exam project training at a pace the individual is comfortable with. It allows the user to only select lessons and topics that needs to be reviewed more carefully and all subjects can be repeatedly reviewed for better mastery of the lessons. In the end, users are actually saving on expenses in terms of travel, accommodations and seminar costs.

PMP and PDU

A PMP certificate is valid only for three years. As soon as you earn your certificate, you would have to add more credited units into your educational background to ensure that you keep yourself certified. This is what PDU or Professional Development Units is all about.

There are a lot of institutes nowadays which offer further PDUs so that you can take care of your PMP credentials. Here are the important topics you must look for as they give you the necessary PDU units you will need.

PDU in Risk Management – This would help empower your skills when it comes to setting out plans within risky conditions. Risks should not hamper your decisions or your power to carry out your tasks.

PDU in MS Project – Since technology is also vital to project management nowadays, you would find the MS Project application a very handy tool. It helps organize the events of your project through a Gantt chart so that you can keep track of what's currently happening. In addition, it also reminds you of the critical tasks still pending.

PDU in Executive Overview – As project manager, you can eventually be promoted to spearhead bigger groups and even a group of executives. As such, you would need the course to give you managerial and executive skills necessary in handling higher positions.

If you want to maintain your PMP, it is vital that you take up these additional units. After all, they are easily available even online so you wouldn't have to worry about any interference it can make with your current work schedule.

Why Get a PMP Practice Exam

Getting a PMP practice exam is as important as getting training courses in project management. Without this, it will be difficult to prepare for actual PMP exams. In choosing the right PMP practice test, it is essential to make sure that it has quality exam content. It should contain all the objectives of Project Management Professional certification test. To have an effective guide choose a practice exam that is written by experts in the industry to ensure the quality of test questions and reference materials.

PMP Practice exam also offers performance based simulations that can provide candidates hands on experience. The practice test questions given are aligned to real exam questions. This will help in reviewing and testing the candidate's comprehension on the objectives of the certification exam. Practice exam also has detailed explanations on the test answers. Other project management training centers and exam providers also give work books that can help students review anytime, anywhere. Score report is one of the major features of practice exam. This will let professionals aim to get higher test results.

Business professionals these days have demanding schedules and enormous workloads. This allows them to have less time to study and train just to get a PMP certification. Computer Based Training (CBT) and practice exam online are convenient options to easily get a Project Management Professional certification. This will let project managers, students and professionals get comprehensive trainings to obtain their PMP certification. Downloading practice exam guarantees candidates in passing the certification test and getting better score results.

Advantages of Downloading PMP Practice Tests

Getting a Project Management Professional (PMP) certification can change a project manager's career. This will definitely help in boosting one's credential and get to the top. In order to be eligible for this prestigious title, an individual must be able to pass the PMP certification test.

These practice tests guarantee to meet the necessary requirements of real PMP exam. This provide test study modes and helps candidates in viewing a comprehensive explanation on the correct answers. Practice tests also provide reference materials to aid students in reviewing important topics. Aside from that, practice tests also give score report where candidates can view their test scores. This will help them aim to get better grades and higher test results.

One of the main objectives of PMP practice test is to simulate real test environment. It provides a timed test which can help professionals practice for the actual PMP exam. There are several practice tests online that offers free practice exam and demos. Candidates must also be cautious on downloading old versions of practice tests online because this can give them inaccurate information that can loose their chances in passing the PMP test.

Passing the PMP test is just the first step in having successful career in project management. Dealing with everyday work loads is another thing. That is why it is important for professionals to train themselves and understand very well the standards, concepts and techniques in PMP. Practice tests are essential tools to reinforce professional's knowledge and skills in project management.

What Do We Mean When We Talk About PMP Prep?

One possible meaning of PMP Prep is that it refers to the PMP exam preparation stage. To adequately prepare for the PMP accreditation exam, we should know first the content of the genuine exam.

The real PMP certification exam is composed of 200 questions, which you can answer using a multiple-choice answer selection format. Out of these 200, twenty five are actually pre-test questions that are eventually employed in the later iterations of the PMP exam itself. However, to a newbie at Project Management accreditation, it is virtually impossible to identify these 25 questions as being pre-test questions. An examinee is only given four hours to finish the whole exam.

If you took the paper version of the PMP exam, you will get your test results within eight weeks at the most. Those who chose the computer-based exam version will get a printout of their test results right after the test is finished. It is up to you which one is preferable for you. Your test results ought to show your total score, as well as how you fared in the different areas of the exam.

So, your PMP prep efforts ought to follow this type of test administration methodology. First, you should know what the coverage of the exam questions will be (not necessarily the specific questions.) Second, you could look for mock PMP exams to practice with. But the value of any mock exam lies with the ability to come up with logical answers under time pressure. So bear in mind that it is you who can adequately understand what you are capable of doing under a limited space of time.

How to Guarantee Adequate PMP Preparation

As with any form of accreditation, adequate PMP Preparation is necessary if the student wants to have or produce a higher score after taking the PMP accreditation exam itself. The PMP certification is concerned with setting the appropriate standards for knowledge and skills in Project Management. This means that anyone who considers himself an expert in Project Management but lacks the technical knowledge as set by the Project Management Institute would still benefit from adequate PMP Preparation anyway.

All PMP preparation methodologies (such as self-study training modules, sample exams, and online training courses) should be able to impart the importance of Project Management, the maturity of Project Management in the key organization, and the PMP certification process itself.

A person aspiring to become a PMP must be well acquainted with how to apply the principles of Project Management as stated within the Project Management Body of Knowledge (PMBOK.) For that matter, this PMP accreditation candidate ought to also know what the ten areas of the PMBOK are. The 44 key processes of the discipline of Project Management should also be considered and absorbed by the student, as well as how they function in conjunction with one another.

It maybe safely said that the PMBOK is a compilation of tried and tested Project Management principles. Even individuals who are aspiring to become PMP consultants rather than simply PMP personnel should have a working understanding of what the PMBOK is all about. Since the Project Management Institute is now the global organization administering Project Management standards, a candidate for PMP would do well to dwell on the PMBOK and its contents as the best form of PMP Preparation there is.

PMP = Project Management

PMP is what true project management is all about. It defines a good project manager in many different ways. How? By simply becoming a benchmark which provides all that is necessary for project managers to know when it comes to carrying out their profession.

Knowledge is not the only thing important with PMP. It also aims to uplift professionals worthy of the term "project manager" by looking at the person's credentials and background information.

Hence, educational background and work experience are being evaluated. These areas help the aspirant's professional character to stand out. These things are necessary for authorities to see how much the aspirant has dedicated when it comes to managing projects and making it a worthwhile career. Through these background checks, authorities would be able to glimpse how dedicated the person would be as a project manager. Here are some of the PMP credentials which are focused on:

- Proven work record in handling responsibility for lengthy projects without the need to be under a certain supervisor. - Documented achievement in handling time-constrained projects with limited resources. - Skills pertaining to in depth knowledge in various project management methodologies.

These credentials are usually seen through the job details which aspirants would present in great detail. These are usually discussed under work experience.

From these credentials, it can be seen that project management is not something that can be done immediately. Project management takes time and maturity for someone to be able to have a full of grasp of its concepts. This is what PMP is really after—certifying an experienced understanding and appreciation of the many facets of project management.

PMP Questions' Objectives

People who are bound to take the PMP certification are also going to take PMP practice tests prior to the actual day of exam. You should definitely do so if you aspire to take the PMP. It is necessary not just so you can familiarize yourself with the entire exam but also as a way of boosting your confidence that you can pass the exam and obtain certification.

Of course, the real concern with PMP is the questions they contain. Although presented in multiple choice formats, the PMP questions can be tactically presented to make the exam a bit more difficult. Actually, these questions are based on the following general objectives:

1. Initiating – PMP questions aim to gauge how innovative you are when it comes to spearheading an original project.

2. Planning – After coming up with an idea, it is only logical to form a feasible plan to suit its implementation. This is what PMP questions pertaining to planning aim to gauge.

3. Execution – No matter how good a plan is and how unique and idea is, it would not come to life if execution was poorly done. Thus, PMP questions also have a bulk to ask about this so that a project manager's influence can also be considered.

4. Control – It is not enough that the plan is already being implemented. Usually, the project will go for a certain period of time. Thus, it is important that a project manager would be able to control all factors which can affect the project.

5. Closing – Although this generally talks about how the project manager ends the project, the PMP questions which pertain to this also highlights the taker's capability to close a project not with finality but as a means of beginning a new one.

How to Get a Positive Result in PMP Test

Project Management Professional (PMP) can provide opportunities and positive results in project manager's career. This will give them a chance to prove to their employer that they deserve to have a promotion and a higher salary. Those who want to have a new career in project management; it is a wise decision to invest on trainings to acquire the PMP certification. This will help them get a head start on the proper concepts, standards and processes in project management.

To pass the requirements in PMP, it is essential to get trainings, practice tests and study guides to equip and prepare candidates in getting a passing result in their test. These preparation tests and courses will help them prepare for the intensive certification exam in PMP. Aside from that, preparation test also provides simulation exams that will allow the students to view test results and let them take the practice test as often as they want.

In real certification exam, candidates can choose a computer based examination that can provide them with test results tight away. That is why getting a simulated preparation test will help candidates in having the confidence to take the examination. This will also help them be familiarized with the topics and give them a view on what to expect in real certification test.To be successful in passing the PMP certification test, it is important to have the necessary tools to aid in studying and preparing for the certification exam. This will absolutely help them getting the right training for the job.

PMP Results: The Best

There are varied results in terms of someone being able to get the desired passing scores in the Certification Examinations for PMP. It is a very hard and difficult Examination to pass. The questions are so many and complex that in terms of the time allotted for the Examination it is simply not enough to begin with. In fact, the answers themselves are the main cause of the mischief for the apparent lack of time.

The answers, or rather the list of answers are all made to give the impression that they are all correct and choosing the best one is deemed to be the hardest task. Also, there are 200 questions, all in all, but 25 of these are dummy questions that have no significant purpose whatsoever other than to confuse and hamper the applicant's question and answer methods. These questions are also made to make the Examination more dangerous than ever.

Past takers, like Ms. Corpuz, says that in the Examination the pressure is so intense that there is little left for errors. It is simply a Certification Examination that is designed to separate the best from the better. In this way, the best are rewarded with the PMP and the better is given the sign that their talents and abilities are still not sufficient enough to pass the Examinations.

This is why the people concerned in the business of Project Management take the results of the PMP very seriously. The PMP is the result of the best being rewarded by the only thing that matters in their kind of business.

PMP Resume: Not a Miracle-Worker

There are a lot of questions on the use of having a Certification. In fact, having one presents a lot more questions than answers. These questions would primarily start or lead to a Certification's use. Most people who have taken the Examination and passed it remark that it is indeed needed.

In fact, many Project Managers would attest to this. One such Project Manager, named as Mr. Magruder, states that his resume was appreciated even more by his future employers. Whenever he would apply for a job, his PMP Certification was a sure way to earn him raised eyebrows and a lead against the other applicants. This is not to say that only a PMP Certification is needed to jumpstart the person's resume.

Although, a having PMP Certification creates the impression that the applicant is able and talented enough to perform for the job, it will still be up to the applicant on how he should bring himself up to being hired. A Certification will only aid him in being considered for the position. In cases where the applicant is already in a company, a PMP Certification would help him to get a promotion more easily than a worker with no Certification.

A Certification will greatly affect the applicant's credibility in front of his future and current employers, like in the case of Mr. Magruder, who greatly impressed his future employers with his credentials and experience coupled by a PMP Certification. The PMP Certification is not a miracle-dose that immediately results to hiring or promotion, rather it just helps in achieving these.

PMP Sample and Predictor

Preparing for any type of licensure or certification exams is a must. Sure there are various methods you can adapt. All of these are proven methods. But, there's also another way of preparing for these types of exams in such a way that you get a good vibe of the looming day.

How? By taking practice tests.

Practice tests allow you to gauge just how prepared you actually are. It gives you a venue for applying whatever information you have gathered from all of your exam reviews.

So if you want to take the PMP certification, practice tests are a great way of giving you a PMP sample.

Practice tests for PMP simulate the actual certification exam. Although simulated, this does not mean that the contents of the practice exam would be similar to that of the actual one. It is just but a PMP sample.

These PMP samples also contain multiple-choice questions. You can also use a predictor while taking it so that you can see how you pace the entire exam and which types of questions do you usually take up some time to answer. All you have to do is have an extra sheet which you would divide into three different columns— 25%, 50%, 90%.

These percentages will become your predictor. For each question, check the right column which corresponds to how sure you are with the answer you chose. Checking 90% means you are sure or have only the slightest bit of doubt with your choice, 50%

would mean that you are unsure, and 25% means you guessed your answer. Skipping numbers would not count in the predictor.

Combine your PMP sample with your own predictor and make that certification a sure thing.

Is it Legal To Use a PMP Sample Test for Exam Preparation?

Is there any harm in using a PMP Sample Test during the exam preparation stage? You might be unpleasantly surprised to find that in some cases, yes, it is wrong to use a PMP Sample Test.

There are some cases now of training institutions of being accused of plagiarism or copyright infringement when relying on the PMBOK (or Project Management Body of Knowledge created by the Project Management Institute which administers the PMP accreditation exam itself.) By using the PMBOK, these training institutions are said to be encroaching on the intellectual property rights of the Project Management Institute which has exclusive rights to content of the PMBOK.

You need to examine the law in the country where the PMP Sample Test was created and even international law regarding copyrights and intellectual property rights to be sure in your own mind what these rights are. Though it is unlikely a student would be slapped with a lawsuit for using a PMP Sample Test of dubious origins, it would still be unpleasant and uncomfortable to use one knowing that it was derived from a business or non profit using deceitful means (if you had a conscience, that is.)

Intellectual property rights are the new field of legal concern which affects present and future Project Management practitioners, but even then intellectual property right infringement or theft is quite difficult to prove and is often judged via subjective means. But to make sure you are getting a good deal, do make it a point to read the original PMBOK of the Project Management Institute then compare it to your PMP Sample Test. This is the only way you can see for yourself the originality of the PMP Sample Test you are about to take.

What to Expect in PMP Student Test Prep for the MS 70-300 Exam

The IT industry has a great need for Project Management Professional (PMP) certified individuals. With its fast growing software industry, it is necessary to have the right skills to manage resources, network systems and communication. To be effective in the job, it is important to have the necessary skills. Professionals and students should constantly initiate improving their knowledge and skills in managing projects. There are student test prep that can help individuals get the necessary preparation for MS 70-300 exam.

This test prep can help IT professionals in getting the necessary trainings and instructions. The MS 70-300 exam prep has 6 hour video training that discusses fundamental knowledge in programming that includes VB.NET and XML. This Computer Based Training in MS 70-300 focuses on recognizing the Microsoft .NET Solution Architecture and Analyzing Requirements. Getting MS 70-300 test prep can provide IT professionals the ability to assess the feasibility of the solution, examine and refining project scope, evaluate business requirements, develop conceptual design and physical design.

In addition to this, MS 70-300 provides skills on creating standards, processes and specifications. In taking this exam, there are no prerequisites needed. The only requirement is to have at least two years of experience in creating documents that identify the needs of software solutions in different business areas. This also includes experience in analyzing the customer needs and designing, implementing and developing solutions. Trainings are very important especially in the IT industry. The PMP student test prep is a wise investment to help IT professionals in passing the MS 70-300 exam.

PMP Test Basics

PMP certification exams are generally computer generated. They are initially made fro the purpose of assessing the test-taker's ability within the following primary aspects of project management:

- Initiation - Planning - Execution - Monitoring and controlling - Closing the project - Acknowledgement of responsibilities—both social and professional

If you want to take the PMP test, you can either fill up the application form included in the PMP Credential Handbook or choose to fill it up online by logging on to the PMI website. The application form would require you to list in detail the PMP eligibility of your accomplishments.

The PMP test contains 200 questions which are all in multiple-choice format. Upon taking it, you will encounter a pretest containing 25 questions. These questions are not going to add up to your overall results. They are just used to help set you off the real course of entering the certification questions.

The questions which would be then evaluated for certification purposes are all made by project management experts. These questions have passed their scrutiny and their approval. To maintain the validity of the questions, they also have to pass psychometric processes. However, the exam is only available in the English language although translation guides are now also developed for foreigners who wish to take the examination. These translation guides must be requested prior to the date of exam.

After taking the exams, a printed result can be obtained to check how well you did on the different categories. The scores are all diagnostic in nature.

Tips on PMP Test Prep

The Project Management Professional certification requires thorough training and study. This can consume a lot of time and money in taking trainings and review. There are a number of sites online that provide PMP Test Prep to candidates.

This will help candidates and professionals to easily prepare for the comprehensive certification exam in project management. The test prep and study guides are important tools in passing the test. Also, this is to help the candidates in training for their future job in project management.

It is proven that with the help of PMP test prep, professionals will not just pass the test but it also provides accurate training to get a promotion and higher salary. Here are some tips on how to prepare for the PMP test:

*   To prepare well for the test, it is important to keep study guides and test prep in accessible places. To kill time, students can bring along these guides wherever they go.

*   Professionals can also avail of Computer Based Training (CBT) course and test prep to effectively study in the office or at home. Anytime, anywhere.

*   Take practice test and aim to make the scores better on each try.

*   Remember in taking tests, it is important to know the nine knowledge areas, five process groups and the 39 component processes.

These tips will help professionals in successfully using their test prep. This will surely enhance their skills and prepare them for their PMP certification. Now getting a better job can be achieved by getting the right preparation for PMP certification.

What to Expect in PMP Training

The Project Management training is an important process in order to pass the certification test. This will help a lot in improving the processes and procedures in managing the projects in software, construction, engineering, automotive and many more. This certification is indeed a good way to start a professional's career in project management.

The PMP training course will benefit project managers to effectively organize limited resources, manage project change, work efficiently to beat the deadlines and improve team performance. The PMP training will help deliver successful plans, manage projects and develop leadership skills in the actual job environment. Aside from that, training can assist professionals in determining schedules and prioritizing tasks without compromising other important assignments. These will surely help the professionals in being an effective leader and project manager.

Getting the necessary trainings vary in different ways. Interested practitioners, project managers and professionals can obtain trainings that will fit their lifestyle. One option can be classroom based training for those who wanted to have instructors to lead the course. Another option is having online trainings that can help hard working professionals get the necessary skills in planning a successful implementation of projects. This includes instructional video training in CD/DVD and simulated exams that will help candidates practice for the PMP exam.

Obtaining trainings in PMP can strengthen the project management skills of professionals. Project managers can get refresher courses to help improve their skills in managing projects. There are various tools that will help candidates and professionals in successfully control and deliver project goals.

Project Management Certification: The Significance of PMBOK

The Project Management Professional certification program is an acknowledged credential to several organizations and businesses worldwide. To be competent in the business industry, it is necessary to have the certification to prove the person's capability. This will help professionals obtain greater opportunities and get a higher salary.

The Project Management certification helps a lot of professionals in realizing their dream and getting a good job. Aside form that, there is a Project Management Body of Knowledge or PMBOK Guide that will help students and practitioners in providing services in Project Management. This certification is ideally for those who wanted to improve their knowledge and skills in creating project control plans, providing suggestions on performance limits, giving support in the administrative disclosure and many more.

The PMBOK Guide provides standards, concepts and knowledge in the proper practices of Project Management. This guide is accepted and approved by the American National Standard (ANS) by American National Standard Institute. This certification program aims to help professionals and students in acquiring the skills needed in order to perform well on the job.

The PMBOK is a process based guide. Initially it has 5 group processes that are usually seen in most projects. These are: Initiating, executing, planning, controlling and monitoring, and closing. In order to obtain this guide, professionals can download it in the internet. Just search for sites that give updated versions to provide an accurate standard in project management. This will also give practitioners and professionals a convenient way to review, study and pass the certification exam.

Why Should I Pursue Project Management PMP PMI Accreditation?

Project Management PMP PMI accreditation is the second tier in a three-rung ladder of Project Management accreditation. The first rung is the CAPM (or Certified Associate in Project Management); while the last rung is the PgMP (or Program Management Professional.)

If you are pursuing the CAPM (or Certified Associate in Project Management) accreditation or the PMP (or Project Management Professional) accreditation, it is advisable for you to read the ANSI standard publication entitled A Guide to the Project Management Body of Knowledge which is now in its third edition.

If, on the other hand, you are aiming for the PgMP (or Program Management Professional) then you are meant to read the standard publication dubbed A Standard for Program Management, which is considered more advanced than the first publication mentioned.

Project Management PMP PMI accreditation is globally recognized so that someone who has trained for this form of accreditation stands a better chance of becoming employed anywhere in the world for Project Management work. Though the steps in Project Management have been clearly defined by the Program Management Institute, unfortunately, there are still quite a few project managers who have not been formally trained in these Project Management concepts or who have even been exposed to them. Sometimes project managers may be trained in PMI standards but then eventually revert back to their old bad habits in management. This only proves that for Project Management PMP PMI accreditation to be fruitful, it has to be practiced continuously and religiously

– otherwise the old management systems are adhered to and the same poor results keep cropping up.

Project Management Professional (PMP): The Second Tier Process

In this world of certifications there's always the hard part of passing the Examinations. In this case, the PMP is a widely and accepted Certification Examination to undergo. In fact, it is a part of a three stage levels of Certification.

For example, a person named Alex took the first stage, which is aptly named as Certified Associate in Project Management (CAPM) is considered to be the first tier, and he passed it. This would then enable him to try out the next stage of Certification Examinations, which is the PMP.

There is however the third and the last of the many and different stages, which is the Project Management Professional (PgMP), which is newly released and is deemed as the hardest. Now Alex may, after passing the PMP, take the PgMP.

There are many benefits that Alex may enjoy in having PMP Certification. One of these is being able to use the abbreviation of PMP right beside their names.

But having one is no mere feat. Aside from the Certification Examinations, the Project Management Institute (PMI) also has a series of stringent requirements that must be passed by the applicant.

Without these requirements, even a passing of the Examinations by Alex would go for naught. In the end, it must be remembered that all of these is necessary as this Certification is mainly a tiered process of ascension from Project Team Members to Program Managers. This is more likely to improve the quality of the takers or applicants than having a one-time Examination. In the PMP, for Alex to become successful in his career, he direly needs to work harder, and of course, achieve better than average or passing Certification Examinations test results.

What are the Requirements to become a Project Manager PMP?

Since Project Management means that a Project Manager will be required to harness all the project resources at his disposal to assure the correct implementation and success of the project in question within the constraints being experienced. This may seem quite a simple thing to assure stakeholders but it is harder than it actually looks.

One reason for difficulties to crop up is that the Project Manager is inadequately trained for this particular project – so that when problems arise, the Project Manager finds himself paralyzed with fear and indecision, afraid to take the risk of pursuing a certain action but equally afraid of making mistakes if he does pursue that course of action.

To be considered for the position of Project Manager PMP, it is necessary to have the necessary background for the job. Some requirements you may need to show proof of are: resident of the area where the project will be undertaken; experience in use and management of a Mainframe environment for a specified period of time; knowledge of and skills in MS Office applications; a proven capacity for leadership of at least five years; additional training in the discipline where Project Management is to be implemented (such as Information Technology) for a certain number of years; and the ability to commit to a contract (whether short term or long term.)

Yes, Information Technology is one field where Project Management is greatly in use and needed right now. If you are a PMP, you may want to bone up on your IT skills; while if you are an IT person, you should do research on what Project Management is.

These two approaches complement one another and help you to gain proficiency in both to make synergistic results happen.

Empower Your Resume With a PMP Certification

If you want to boost your career in project management, you would have to start with creating a powerful resume.

A PMP certificate can possibly open more doors for you. The certificate is only given to individuals who have passed a strict screening process. The certificate gives credit for how much you know about the ins and outs of project management Before you can be allowed to take the exam certification, you would have to pass first assessment which seeks to gauge just how much credible educational experience as well as work expertise you have had.

What's best is that you also get additional perks by becoming a PMI member. You get to have a bigger network of people connected to various industries. What's more is that all of them are in the same position as yours. This can also help open more doors for you if you want to go ahead and explore other industries which are also available out there for you.

Recruitment people of consider your credentials as they look at your resume. However, a PMP certificate accessorizes your resume and adds further credibility to you and your chosen profession. It gives the impression that you truly are committed and dedicated with project management since you opted to undergo the said certification program.

A resume is your best ticket in bagging the job you want. Chances are, a lot of people are also going to compete with you for that coveted job. To ensure that your resume boasts of something extraordinary, get that PMP certification and watch those calls come in to invite you for an interview.

Real benefit from PMP certification

Apart from 'foot in the door' help it provides in jobsearch, what else is the benefit in having a PMP certification (if your company doesn't insist on it)? Passing the exam doesn't prepare one for real life project management challenges, but does PDU accumulation help?

PDUs are measuring units PMI uses to quantify professional activities relating to Project Management - and one should accumulate 60 PDUs every 3 years to continue to be a "PMP in good standing"

Certification programs, particularly those with continuing education requirements, serve multiple purposes:

- they do, as you noted, provide a foot-in-the-door service by (rightly or wrongly) giving the hiring entity a place to start in determining what the candidate may know

- they also provide you with education/knowledge/skills that will serve help you (and therefore your company) in stepping up to those real life project management challenges

- and, additionally, they provide you with an incentive to continue growing your knowledge and acquiring new knowledge/skills as real life challenges also change

What is the RMC PMP Exam Prep System?

The RMC Project Management company was founded by Rita Mulcahy and is a company that aims to undertake professional development and Project Management training of students who enroll with them. RMC Project Management has become an institution in the industry since it has trained many thousands of project management professionals in its 15 years of existence.

The RMC PMP Exam Prep System tries to be different from other PMP exam training organizations in that students will get a shorter training time under RMC Project Management company. The training you get in RMC Project Management company emphasizes knowledge retention and training communication, that can be applied in real world conditions as well.

Rita Mulcahy also developed a book on Project Management training herself – entitled the PMP Exam Prep book. Other books produced by Rita Mulcahy were awarded the Professional Development Product of the Year award by the Project Management Institute.

Training under the RMC Project Management company can take as little as half a day or as long as a whole week (depending on how necessary it is.) You can even have training sessions customized if you prefer.

Another service from the RMC Project Management company would be the e-Learning courses available via the Internet. This service is apt for those who may be on the go constantly or are in remote locations accessible only through online means.

Project managers who are destined in over 40 countries have been able to utilize the RMC Project Management company services to date.

Printed in the United States
117248LV00006B/73/P